LIFE SKILLS FOR TEENS

Becoming Your Best Self: Practical Tips for Developing Your Personality, Navigating the World, Building Strong Relationships, and Designing Your Future

Uncovering the 8th Most Common Mistakes Teens Make That Could Ruin Their Future

MICHAEL WOODS

DISCLAIMER:

The information provided in this book is intended to be educational and geared towards young adults. It is not a substitute for professional advice or personalized guidance tailored to your individual circumstances. The author and publisher are not responsible for any actions taken by readers based on the information presented in this book. Every effort has been made to ensure the accuracy of the information provided, but the author and publisher cannot guarantee that the information is complete, accurate, or up-to-date. The success of implementing the life skills and advice presented in this book will depend on the individual's personal situation, choices, and actions. The author and publisher disclaim any liability for any loss, damage, or injury caused by the use or reliance on the information provided in this book. Readers should seek the advice of a qualified professional before making any decisions or taking any actions based on the information presented in this book.

FREE GIFT JUST FOR YOU!

Our comprehensive career guide will help you find a fulfilling career path that aligns with your desired lifestyle. Discover a wealth of diverse job options, practical business startup advice, unique and exciting business ideas, as well as valuable college degrees that are worth the investment.

Download NOW for exclusive access to these insights.

Or go to http://michaelwoodslife.com/

TABLE OF CONTENTS

INTRODUCTION

Welcome to a unique stage in your life. If you're reading this book, it means you're between the ages of 14 and 20. You should know that you're in a unique time in history. Things are very different now than in most of human history, and being a teenager these days is not easy. This book is about giving you the knowledge you need to succeed in many areas of life. You want what we all want: to be healthy, to be successful with finances, to have a good social circle that cares about us, such as family, friends, romance, etc., and to be happy. We all have to face challenges, but if you are well-informed, things will be easier for you. We will give you the guidance you need to face the challenges we all have to face.

You probably think what happens to you now depends mostly on external circumstances like your parents, what society expects, etc. But let me tell you, the older you get, the more control you have over your life. You're in complete control of the direction your life takes. Where you will be at 25, 35, or 45 years old is totally up to you. Not only are we going to cover the issues teens face today, but we also will be talking about the things that will matter when you are an adult, such as money, the current education system, social skills, friendship, relationships, how to find your career and your purpose, how the world works, and how to get the most out of it, and much more. The knowledge you will gain from this book will guide you toward success no matter what you want out of life.

We are going to give you the eight most common mistakes young people make that negatively affect their future. Common mistakes that most of us have made one or the other. You are early in this journey of life, so you can prevent a lot of things from happening to you if you start catching up early on the things you shouldn't do or should avoid and if, at the same time, you do the things that most people don't do, you will live the life that most people won't. Many of the problems we face are common to many others.

This is a unique and exciting stage of your life. You are starting to make decisions of your own and explore new interests; you are preparing to be an adult and a productive member of society. But with all of these new freedoms and opportunities come challenges and responsibilities. Our goal is to help you develop the skills and give you the knowledge and confidence you need to navigate today's world and achieve your goals.

If you don't know what your goals are yet, that's totally fine and normal as well. We will be talking about how to find what it is you want to do in life, and for this, you need to know yourself and visualize the lifestyle you want. Whether you are just starting out on your life's journey or are well on your way, this book is for you. Everyone has the potential to succeed, and we hope these pages will provide you with the tools and guidance you need to make the most of your life. There is a lot of excitement and challenges ahead. In a few years, you will be living independently and have to decide what you will do in your mid-20s. The decisions we make now affect our future; think about it. You are where you are now because of the actions and decisions you made in the past. And where you will be at 25 or 35 years old will be the product of the decisions and actions you take every day from now on periodically for the next years. So let's get started! Together, we will explore the life skills you need to succeed and pave the way for a bright and rewarding future.

CHAPTER 1

TOO YOUNG TO BE AN ADULT. TOO OLD TO BE A KID

Welcome to the wild world of social media, where everything is on display for the world to see. It's hard to imagine what life was like before the internet and smartphones, but trust me; it was very different. As a teenager in today's world, you're navigating a unique set of challenges that previous generations did not have to face. On the one hand, you have access to technology and opportunities that are beyond what anyone could have imagined a few decades ago. You can connect with people worldwide, learn anything you want, and explore new interests with just a few clicks. But on the other hand, life can feel pretty overwhelming at times. You're expected to do well in school, get involved in extracurricular activities, and fit in with your peers, all while dealing with the pressures of social media and online communication. Building meaningful relationships and finding true friends and romance in this fast-paced, ever-connected world can be difficult. It may seem like we're more connected than ever, but in many ways, we're more disconnected than ever before.

So, you have opportunities that previous generations could only dream of, but you also have to navigate a world that can be pretty overwhelming.

Do you feel like being a teen/ young adult can sometimes be:

- Competitive
- Confusing
- Fast
- Stressful
- Materialistic
- Pressured
- Different
- Rustle
- Crazy
- Messy
- Scary
- Rushed

Being a teenager or young adult can be a real rollercoaster ride with ups and downs. And let's be honest, figuring out who you are and what you want in life can be pretty confusing. Everything seems to be happening so quickly, and it can be hard to keep up with all the information and opportunities that come your way while you are still figuring things out.

The Challenges You Encounter

Being a teenager in today's world is tough, really tough. You've got high school, a job, sports, friends, and all these other things you want to do. Being an adult, at least you get to choose how to spend 8 hours of your day. You're getting way more pressured than ever before.

We're asking you to do too much with not enough time. It's chaotic, tiring, mind-blowing, conflicting, and contradictory at times. And it's not just school; you've got extra activities like a job, family stuff, and extracurriculars, and you might feel like you don't have enough time for yourself. It's frustrating because you're often dismissed for being too young and inexperienced. Living with uncertainty is something you've probably gotten used to without even realizing it. So you're trying to party with friends, trying to finish high school with good grades, and your future is something that you think you'll figure out on the way. It's harder to enjoy your friends and be a teenager at a slower pace because you are being pulled in so many directions that you find yourself living at a fast pace, and this wasn't always the case. There is so much information out there; whatever you want to find is out there. Everything is so accessible, leaving you confused about what information to pick up. Social media platforms like Facebook, Instagram, Snapchat, and Twitter did not exist 20 years ago. Teenagers had to develop relationships face to face when they saw each other, so they did not have the same level of connectivity and constant communication with their peers that teenagers have today. You were a lot less under the microscope, relationships were more organic, and because of that reason, it was easier to make friends and enjoy these teenage years at a slower pace, being with friends, hanging out, and not having to be so overwhelmed with stuff. You're dealing with a lot of pressure to do well in school and plan for your future, all while trying to figure out who you are and what you want in life. And let's not forget about social media and screens that are always around and the mental health struggles that come with it. But it's important to remember that this is a time of growth and change for you. And with the right support and understanding from adults, you can overcome any challenges that come your way. Let's dive into some of the big problems facing teens today and how to tackle them.

Growing Up In The Age Of Social Media:

Being a teenager in today's world means you're living in a time when technology and social media are everywhere. It's normal to have a smartphone and be active on social media, but it also means that you're being watched and monitored more than ever before. With the ability to take photos and videos easily and share them with a big audience, it can feel like your every move is being recorded and judged. You're not alone in feeling this way; it's something many teens deal with today. Keep in mind that you always have control over what you share online, and think carefully before posting something that could be misinterpreted or used against you.

Here are a few tips for being more mindful and safe when using technology and social media as a teenager:

- Be aware of your privacy settings: Make sure you understand the privacy settings of the apps and platforms you use and adjust them accordingly. Limit the information you share to only people you know and trust.
- Think before you post: Before you post anything online, think about how it could be perceived by others. Once people see it, it can't be unseen.
- Don't share personal information: Be careful about sharing personal information, such as your phone number, address, or school name. Scammers and predators can use this information to find and harm you.
- Be selective about who you add/follow: If you don't know the person in real life, think twice before accepting their request.
- Take a break: If you're feeling overwhelmed or stressed by the constant presence of technology and social media, take a break. Put your phone down and spend some time offline.

Keep in mind that social media is not a complete representation of reality. People often present a curated version of themselves online; they only show their highlight reels, not the whole picture. It is important to maintain a healthy perspective and not compare yourself to others. You're unique and special and should not feel pressured to fit in. Instead of trying to conform to the expectations of others, focus on your own values and goals. It's okay to be different and to embrace your unique qualities and characteristics. Practice self-acceptance and be true to yourself, even if this means standing out or being different from others. Remember that you can always come to someone you trust for support and encouragement when you are feeling pressure to fit in.

Different types of social pressure you may encounter:

Being a teenager in today's world can be tough, with pressures coming from all directions. From fitting in with your peers to performing well in school, from conforming to beauty standards to figuring out what you want to do with your life, it can feel like there are a lot of expectations on your shoulders. But it's important to remember that you're not alone in feeling this way.

There are all kinds of pressure from everywhere, like from your peers, your family, and even society as a whole.

Here are a few examples:

Fitting in and being accepted by your peers: Sometimes it feels like you gotta be a certain way or do certain things just to be part of the crowd. It can be tough to stand out and be the way you just are.

Looking a certain way and conforming to beauty standards: There are all kinds of images and expectations thrown at you about how you should look. It can be tough not to compare yourself to others and feel good in your own skin.

Doing well in school and getting into a good college: The pressure to do well in school and get into a good college can be intense. It's hard not to stress out about it all.

Being well-rounded and participating in extracurricular activities: Sometimes it feels like you gotta do a million things just to stand out. It's hard to balance everything and not burn out.

Having a successful future career: There's pressure to know what you want to do with your life and be successful at it. It's hard to know what you want and not stress about the future.

Being on social media and having a positive online image: It can feel like you gotta be online all the time and present a perfect image of yourself. It's hard not to compare yourself to others and stress about it.

Having a romantic partner and being sexually active: There's pressure to be in a relationship or be sexually active. It's hard to know what you want and not feel pressure from others.

Being politically and socially aware and having strong opinions: It can feel like you gotta have all the answers and be an expert on everything going on in the world. It's hard to know what you believe and not stress about it.

Being financially independent and responsible: With the cost of living and education going up, it can feel like you gotta have all your financial sh*t together. It's hard not to stress about it.

Emotional: Dealing with stress, anxiety, and the emotional rollercoaster that comes with being a teenager.

Physical: Keeping your body healthy and dealing with the changes of puberty.

Family: Navigating relationships with your family and dealing with any conflicts or changes that come up.

Do not worry; it is unlikely that you will have to deal with all these issues at once or at all. Not everyone experiences all of these social pressures. It depends on your special circumstances. It can feel like there are a lot of expectations on your shoulders but don't worry, you are not perfect, and you are not supposed to excel in everything. Making progress is what matters. Since you know what to expect now, do not let these pressures overwhelm you. You're still figuring things out, and that's okay. One of the problems with the school system is that we have a system where you either fail or pass, and you have to pass every grade when you are not going to be good at everything. Finally, remember to take care of yourself emotionally and physically by developing healthy habits such as regular exercise, a balanced diet, and getting enough sleep. The better you feel, the better you perform. In conclusion, don't let the social pressures get to you, you're not alone, and you're not supposed to be perfect. Embrace your individuality, build a support system, take control of your online presence, manage stress and anxiety, and take care of yourself. You got this, and remember; it is not about perfection is about progress.

The Huge Advantages You Have:

Let me tell you this. You have opportunities that are unique to this time. You are at a stage in your life where you are starting to gain more independence and autonomy, so you need to know that the opportunities and resources that you have at your disposal these days are insane. You are so lucky that you were born in this unique time in history because it is easier than ever to take complete control of your future and do whatever it is you want and make a living out of it. Generation X, baby boomers, and even millennials did not have the opportunity to have the internet and the ability to achieve the life you want in a way easier way. Now I want to congratulate you on something. You are reading this book right now. This means you are taking investing in yourself and taking action to understand how the world works. Great job. Keep reading. I promise you that reading this book until the end won't disappoint you.

Advantage #1: You have more access to information than ever before.

Before the internet, getting information meant going to the library, reading books, or watching television. This process was often time-consuming and difficult, and finding the information you needed was not always easy. With today's tools like Google and YouTube, you can learn how to do almost anything that doesn't require a degree; you can learn almost anything you want. These resources are incredibly powerful and can provide you with great information on almost any topic you can think of. You have access to vast information at your fingertips; use these tools to your advantage. There is very little wondering these days. Since you have access to all of this information, you can deeply research your interests and easily become informed about a topic. Previous generations did not have this privilege.

Some of the ways teens can take advantage of the access to the information we have today:

- Learning new skills: Before the internet, you did not have the chance to learn new things that easily. Today, you can use the internet to access a wide variety of resources to learn new skills. For example, online tutorials and courses can teach teens how to code, design websites, code, music production, photography, and video editing, just to name a few. So, you have the ability to learn almost anything you want, of course, a skill that can be learned and that doesn't require a degree to perform. Online resources, such as e-books, videos, and podcasts, can also be used to learn new languages, study for exams, or improve writing skills. Some popular platforms for learning new skills online include YouTube, Codecademy, Khan Academy, Coursera, and Udemy.

- Staying informed: It is a lot easier now to stay informed about anything you want. Before, you only had newspapers, television, and radio. Now, the internet provides teens with access to a vast amount of information from a variety of sources, and they can follow social media accounts that provide reliable information on topics they are interested in. Additionally, teens can use the internet to fact-check information they come across and research the credibility of sources before trusting the information. Teens can stay informed about current events and global issues by reading news articles and following social media accounts that provide reliable information.

- Finding opportunities: The internet provides teens with a wealth of opportunities to explore and pursue their interests and passions. Teens can use the internet to research and find internships, summer jobs, and part-time work that align with their skills and interests. Many companies and organizations have online job portals where teens can find and apply for job opportunities. Additionally, teens can use the internet to research, apply to colleges and universities, and explore scholarship opportunities. Websites like LinkedIn, Glassdoor, and Indeed can also be great resources for teens to explore job and internship opportunities.

Advantage# 2: It is easier than ever to live the life you want

If you had grown up at any other time in history, you would have been more confined to a lifestyle that may not have been in your plans. Building wealth and creating the lifestyle you wanted was much harder. You would have had to adapt to social constructs, and if you didn't, there was a high chance you would not have done well. If you were born in poverty, it would have been much harder to get out. You would have been confined to live the typical lifestyle of going to school, then going to college to work a corporate job, climbing the corporate ladder, buying a house in the suburbs, and maybe retiring one day. Don't get me wrong; there is nothing wrong with those things. It's just not for everybody. Since access to information and resources was more limited, it was harder to find and take advantage of opportunities to build wealth. It was also harder to connect and do business with people from all over the world and for people to start and run their own businesses. There was no such thing as remote working, and you did not have the opportunity to earn and work from any location that you desired. While it was still possible to live the life you wanted back in the 70s, 80s, 90s, etc. The internet has greatly expanded the opportunities for people to build wealth and create their desired lifestyle by providing universal access to information and giving everyone the opportunity to achieve their financial goals and live the life they want. The internet has democratized access to information, resources, and opportunities, making it easier for people to take control of their lives and build the future they desire. So, be grateful that you were born in these times when it comes to that.

Advantage #3: You are Free Of Family Responsibilities:

This one is a big one. You are still free from the many responsibilities that come with adulthood. Most of you still live with your parents, who take care of many of the daily expenses, such as rent, bills, and groceries. Additionally, you likely do not have to worry about supporting a family or dealing with the responsibilities of having children. This means you have more time and financial resources to focus on your growth and development. With less economic pressure on your shoulders, you have the ability to invest your time and resources in figuring out what you want to do with your life.

You can explore your interests and passions and take the time to figure out what career path is the best fit for you. This will give you a head start on your future and make the transition to adulthood smoother. You can use this time to build up your financial security. You can work on building your credit score, start saving money, and learn how to manage your finances. This will set you up for success as you move into adulthood and begin to take on more responsibilities. It's important to remember that the choices you make now will affect the rest of your life, so make the most of this time and use it to set yourself up for success in the future. It's also important to note that not everyone has the privilege of living with their parents and having them take care of the daily expenses. It's important to be aware of your own privilege and try to make the most of the resources and opportunities available to you.

Advantage # 4: You have time

You are young! Time is on your side. There is no reason to be stressed about what to do with your future; you have time to figure it out, and this book will help you do that. It doesn't mean you have to relax, but you have your whole life ahead of you. Many of you have not learned the value of time yet, and unfortunately, you are wasting it. Most people admit when they hit their mid-30s that, they wasted their 20s. Don't let that be you. You have time, but don't waste it. If you could travel in time when you are in your 30s, one of the things that you would tell yourself is the importance of understanding time and using it to achieve the goals you have. You are focused on partying and having a good time, and that is fine. You should do that, but at the same time, start working towards the lifestyle you want to have when you are 25-35 years old. Think about it. If you do certain things in your 20s, working towards whatever goal, career, or lifestyle you want, depending on what it is that you want, it may take five years, ten years, or a lifetime, but use it in your favor. You will be amazed at the things you can do by just showing up and doing your best. Show up, do your best, and call it a day. Step by step, you can get ahead. Understand the value of time. You are at a special time in your life where you have the opportunity to explore your passions, try new things, and discover who you are and what you want in life. Embrace this time and make the most of it!

Advantage # 5: There Are a Lot Of Mistakes You Didn't Make Then

As a teenager, you are in a unique position because you have not yet made many of the mistakes that many adults have made. If you take the time to learn from the mistakes of others and make a conscious effort to avoid them, you can put yourself in a very favorable position in your mid-20s to early 30s. Many young adults are not doing that well. Many of them are in debt, with unfulfilling jobs/careers, and in situations that are not really that favorable; all this results from common mistakes that young people make that affect their success later in life. For example, if you learn to manage your finances responsibly, you can avoid debt and build a solid financial foundation. If you learn to make smart career choices, you can set yourself up for success in your chosen field. Additionally, if you learn to establish a good credit history and network, you can open doors to many opportunities in the future. By being proactive and learning from the mistakes of others, you can set yourself up for a successful and fulfilling future. The internet can be a valuable tool in this process, as it provides access to a wealth of information and resources that can help you make informed decisions. Take advantage of the resources available to you, and make the most of your teenage years. With the right knowledge and mindset, you can achieve your goals and create the life you want.

Introduction To The 8th Mistakes:

As young people, we are full of potential and energy, ready to take on the world. However, it's important to be aware that the decisions we make in our teenage and early adult years can significantly impact our lives later on. Unfortunately, many young people make mistakes that are actually very common and affect their future in a negative way. Some of these mistakes can last a decade, and they can range from financial mismanagement, poor career choices, and unhealthy relationships. It's essential to be aware of these common mistakes so that we can take steps to avoid them and set ourselves up for a successful and fulfilling future. This article will explore eight of the most common mistakes young people make and how they can affect their lives later in life. We will discuss topics such as financial management, career development, relationships, and personal growth. By understanding these common mistakes and learning to avoid them, we can take control of our lives and create the future we want. It's also important to remember that everyone's journey is different, and it's okay to make mistakes; the important thing is to learn from them and move forward. By understanding these common mistakes and learning to avoid them, we can take control of our lives and create the future we want.

MISTAKE#1: Not Valuing Time And Wasting It

We all make this mistake, adults too. Unfortunately, teens tend to do it more. Many young people waste their time on activities that don't contribute to their long-term goals or well-being. They spend hours on social media, playing video games, partying, and drinking. There is nothing wrong with doing these things. The problem is when you make that your lifestyle and do it all the time. Some teens get into hard drugs and start having substance abuse problems instead of working on personal projects or developing new skills. Most people admit that they really did not start doing much in many aspects of life until they were in their late 20s or early 30s. And by the time they get or if they get some of the results they were looking for or have a life that they are somehow comfortable with, they are around their late 30s or early 40s, and they realize they could have done it much sooner. it is a horrible feeling when you get where you want to be at 45 when you could have enjoyed that much younger. Wasting time prevents young people from achieving their goals, doing things they really don't want to do, and leads to feelings of regret and dissatisfaction later in life. You have to realize that if you start learning how the world works now, investing in yourself, and starting things accordingly to build the lifestyle you want, by the time you are 25, you can be in an extraordinary situation. Healthy, debt-free, good income, and on the path to a greater life than most people won't and still very young. Time is on your side, have fun party, that is ok, but also it is important to set priorities and to be mindful of how we spend your time. Combine that with knowledge and action. You will be unstoppable. Who knows where you can be when you are 25-30 years old? It is totally fine to party, play video games, hang out with friends, and just be on social media. The problem is when you let it consume your days, your weeks, and your years and don't do anything else. If you waste a lot of time in low-value activities when you don't realize it, you are 30 years old and have very little to show for it.

CHAPTER 2

LET'S UNDERSTAND MONEY

MISTAKE #2: Not Understanding, Or Not Even Bothering To Understand, Money.

Luckily for you, after reading this chapter, you'll be less likely to commit this mistake. But let's face it, a lot of people - including young adults - don't really get money. Many young people take a hands-off approach to their finances, failing to educate themselves about basic financial concepts such as the nature of money, income vs expenses, budgeting, saving, investing, and credit, among others. This lack of understanding can lead to a host of financial problems, including high levels of debt, poor credit scores, and lack of money on a daily basis, and all this leads to difficulty achieving long-term financial goals. When you don't have at least a basic understanding of money, you are making your life harder. Do not let this be you; when you don't bother to understand the money, you are more likely to make poor financial decisions that can hold you back from doing what you really want in *life. Always having money to do want you want doesn't have to be a mystery. Young people may feel trapped in jobs they don't like or unable to pursue their passions because they lack the financial resources to do so. They view money the wrong way, don't understand its nature, and act impulsively. Your poor financial decisions are very costly in the long run when it doesn't have to be that way. If you bother to learn to understand how this tool works, you will learn to have a healthy relationship with it and not make so many mistakes. These mistakes can be really costly, trust me; look around you and see how most people live with unbearable amounts of debt and they have an unhealthy relationship with money. Don't let that be you. Keep reading this cheaper to get the correct perspective on this tool.*

One of the things the school system is failing at is preparing students financially and teaching them about money. Schools should regularly be teaching students things like credit, banking, saving, investing, debt, and student loans, among other things. In this chapter, we will dive into the world of personal finance and teach you the skills and knowledge you need to navigate the financial landscape. This chapter aims to equip you with the tools and understanding you need to make informed financial decisions and set yourself up for a successful financial future. It's unfortunate that the public education system is failing to prepare students for the realities of personal finance. Many students graduate without a basic understanding of how to manage their money, leaving them vulnerable to financial mistakes and setbacks. However, with the information and guidance provided in this chapter, you will be able to take control of your financial future and make informed decisions that will benefit you in the long run. We understand that financial literacy can be daunting, but we promise to make it as clear and easy to understand as possible. With the knowledge you gain here, you'll be able to avoid the common financial mistakes that many young people make and set yourself up for a secure and prosperous future.

Money Is A Tool, Not The Goal:

Let's start with the basics of understanding money. Money is just a tool that you use to get whatever you want: a plane ticket, meal, clothes, car, house, or even fun. Everything we have is a product of money. Just look at your bedroom or house; the furniture and appliances in your home are all products of money. Go outside, and you'll see that the roads, cars, houses, buildings, and infrastructure were all created with money.

If you understand the philosophical nature of money and you see it from the perspective that it is just a tool to get what you want, you can focus more on using it for what you need and enjoy life more. You will change your relationship with it and focus more on providing value to the world by pursuing your desired career rather than chasing paper. You can use it to achieve the things you really want in life rather than letting it consume your thoughts and dictate your actions.

The idea of having enough money to achieve our goals and live a comfortable life is a powerful motivator for many people, but don't let it consume you. The money that you have depends on what you put out to the world. Meaning the frequency with which money comes to us depends on the value that we put into society. When you have a job and you work, there is a certain value that you are providing for compensation. The same is true when you have a business; whatever product or service you provide is a value that is exchanged with money. So the more valuable we are and the more value we provide to society, the more money we can earn.

For example, doctors, engineers, and other skilled professionals typically earn more than unskilled workers. This is because society values their skills and services more highly. Skilled labor will always beat non-skilled labor. That's why there are people out there who aren't much smarter or more talented than you, but they know a few special things that you don't know that allow them to make more money than you right now. Similarly, entrepreneurs who create innovative products or services that improve people's lives can also earn more money.

So, there is something that you need to be doing for money to come to you. You will be broke if you're lazy and don't do much with your life. If you're working a skilled labor job, you won't be broke unless you have bad spending habits, of course. When your income is low, you have to increase the value you put into the world, either by getting a better job or doing something that is more valuable that can make you more money.

How To Stop Being Broke All The Time:

Being broke when you are young is very common. I am sure you have heard the term "broke college student." There are a lot of young people who are completely broke; they feel completely defeated in life, and they feel that money or having more money will fix a lot of these problems they are having, and they are correct. Let's just say this: Not having money sucks. It really sucks. Money is a form of power, a tool to use for what you need. You need to provide for yourself, and when you don't have enough of it, you struggle to make ends meet, and this is not a good feeling.

Most people are broke most of the time, and this is often due to a combination of bad decisions made with money in the past and discrepancies between how much they make and how much they spend. One of the main reasons many people are broke is that they don't have good spending habits; they buy things they don't need and live a life in debt due to being overly materialistic.

When you are young, your income is typically low. You may be in college or working an entry-level job, which doesn't pay much. The key to not being broke when you are young is to make as much money as possible and spend as little as possible. This means not buying expensive cars, not going out as much, keeping your entertainment expenses low, and just don't buy unnecessary stuff. Keep your spending in line with your income.

You have control over your income and spending. You can choose to keep a job where you make a certain amount of money or look for a job where you can make more. You choose how you spend your money day by day, month by month, and year by year. Live simpler and spend wiser. If you do this, you are not going to be broke all the time.

Minimalism:

Have you ever seen those families who have so much stuff that not only do they pack their whole garage, but they also need to rent storage to store everything? Eighty percent of those things are probably stuff they will never use. This is often referred to as "self-storage." Having this much stuff brings headaches and stress to these families more than joy. Having so much stuff everywhere makes them feel overwhelmed by their possessions, and they struggle to find space for everything in their homes.

Minimalism is a lifestyle and philosophy that emphasizes simplicity and the elimination of unnecessary possessions. It is about living with less and focusing on what is most important to you, saving money, and being purpose-focused in the meantime. It is a lifestyle and mindset where the focus is on living with fewer material possessions and simplifying one's life. It involves removing unnecessary items and simplifying one's living space and possessions to focus on what truly matters. This brings meaning to your life. Minimalism is often associated with decluttering, downsizing, and simplifying one's home and possessions, but it can also include simplifying one's schedule, relationships, and overall lifestyle. The goal is to live a more intentional life, free from the clutter and distractions of excess possessions, and to focus on what truly brings happiness and fulfillment.

So, be more critical of your purchases, and don't clutter your home with stuff. There is no need to buy the newest car or get the newest piece of furniture. There is no need to buy random stuff that you will probably not use. There is no need to eat out all the time. When it comes to objects, ask yourself, "Do I use this, or do I want this?" Try to find what really serves your purpose in your life. It's all about living simply and having only what you need to go about your daily life. This makes it much easier to focus on your purpose and also saves a lot of money by reducing impulsive and unnecessary spending.

Because your income is expected to be low during your teenage years and early 20s, the best way to avoid being broke is to be smart with your spending.

Here are different ways you can do that and things to avoid:

- Prioritize your spending: Make a list of what you need to spend money on, like school supplies or clothes, and what you don't need to spend money on, like eating out or buying the latest trendy clothes. Prioritizing your spending will help you make sure you're not overspending on things you don't need. It is easier to have control over materialistic things than non-materialistic like entertainment.
- Set specific financial goals: It's important to have a plan for your money and know what you want to achieve. For

example, if you want to save up for a car or a trip, setting a specific financial goal will help you focus on what you need to save for and make sure you're not wasting money on unnecessary things. What typically happens when we buy things we don't need is we have less money and more stuff we don't use, which can clutter our homes and make it harder to find and enjoy the things we do need. This can lead to feelings of guilt, regret, or dissatisfaction, especially when we realize that we spent money on something that we don't even use or like.

- Eliminate unnecessary expenses: Take a look at your typical expenses. Are you constantly spending money on things you don't need? For example, if you're paying for a subscription that you're not using or a club membership you're not interested in, cancel it and save that money. The most common unnecessary expenses teens have are:

- Cook more, eat out less: Eating out at restaurants or fast food chains every day or more than twice per week can be a big expense. It is totally ok to do it sometimes, not a big deal, but if you do it more than three times per week, it is a problem. Eat out less and cook more at home.

- Clothes and shoes: Teens often feel pressure to keep up with the latest fashion trends, which makes them overspend on clothes and shoes. There is no need to do that. have a nice wardrobe but don't go to the extreme of having to feel you need to dress differently every day.

- Entertainment: This is one of the biggest expenses young adults have. If they are socially active, they tend to go out often, and all of those activities add up quickly. Going out with your friends and having a social life is important BUT try to spend the least possible. If you are able to control much of the spending in other areas, you can probably be a little less careful here since this is your social life and it is important.

- Technology: Teens often want the latest gadgets and devices, such as smartphones, laptops, and gaming consoles, which can be a significant expense. If you need it, go ahead, but if you don't need it, there is no need to have the latest iPhone, the latest iMac, or the latest tablet.

- Subscription services: Teens may also spend money on subscription services such as streaming platforms, gaming services, or other online subscriptions. They probably have all streaming platforms and only use one or 2. Why spend money on things you don't watch? Cut it out.

- Avoid impulse buying: It's easy to see something you want and buy it without thinking, but impulse buying can add up quickly and leave you with things you don't need or even regret buying. Next time you're tempted to buy something, take a step back and think about whether you really need or you just want it.

- Live with less: Try to live with less, in terms of possessions, and see how it makes you feel. You might find that living with less can bring more freedom and joy to your life. It's not about being austere or denying yourself things but more about being intentional with what you have and what you bring into your life. It doesn't mean living in deprivation or denying oneself of things. It's about being intentional with what we bring into our lives and ensuring that what we have brings value, joy, and purpose.

Here are some of the benefits of living with less:

- Increased freedom: When we have fewer possessions, we have less to worry about and take care of, which can free up time and energy for other things. This can help us focus on

24

what truly matters and prioritize the things that bring us joy and fulfillment. Trust me; you feel more free.

- More clarity and focus: Having less clutter in our homes and lives can help us think more clearly and make better decisions. It allows us to focus on what truly matters and prioritize the things that bring us joy and fulfillment.

- Reduced stress: Being surrounded by clutter and having too many possessions can be overwhelming and stressful, and also it takes time to organize so much stuff all the time. Simplifying our possessions can help reduce stress and anxiety since we have a lot less to worry about.

- Increased creativity: When we have fewer possessions, we have fewer distractions and can focus better. Keeping your place clean and organized is a lot easier. This can lead to increased creativity, productivity, and inspiration.

- More savings: By not buying unnecessary things and not spending money on things we don't need, we can put money towards more important things like saving for education, traveling, or investing in something that can bring more long-term benefits.

- A sense of purpose: When we live with less, we are forced to be more intentional with our possessions and focus on what truly matters. This can bring a sense of purpose and fulfillment to our lives.

- Positive impact on the environment: Minimalism also encourages being mindful of our consumption, not just in terms of material possessions but also in terms of energy, water, and other resources. By consuming less, we can reduce our impact on the environment.

To finish this section, minimalism is a lifestyle choice that can bring a multitude of benefits to your life. I am only giving you the knowledge of this; you don't have to be a minimalist. But if you choose to live simpler, your life will be a lot easier in almost every way.

MISTAKE # 3 Rush Into Buying A New Car

When buying a new car, not necessarily brand new, but a new one for you, don't rush the purchase due to excitement. You have to be smart when purchasing a vehicle because making the wrong decision and buying a car the wrong way can have severe consequences for your near future. You can screw yourself for the next 3-5 years. For example, if you buy a "lemon" with a high-interest loan, you can get yourself into a nightmare. And that is just one way. Before making a purchase, it's essential to think and keep several things in mind. It can be easy to get caught up in the excitement and spend more money than you had planned. Don't make your life miserable in the next 3-5 years.

Cars are a necessary mode of transportation for most people, taking them from home to work and vice versa. They are also a financial responsibility that requires maintenance and also depreciates in value over time. Look at the long term consecuences of your purchase. Your car payment and insurance are typically your second highest expenditure after rent and, combined, can EASILY be well over $600 a month. If you don't handle this correctly, this can significantly impact your ability to build wealth long-term.

So don't buy a car without knowing all the terms of the loan; you make sure you can make the payment and the vehicle will be reliable. We are going to give you specific advice next.

How Cars Keep You Poor. The Smart Way Of Owning A Vehicle:

Even if you are a car person, you will find this valuable because I am not telling you that you shouldn't own a car or buy a lemon. I want to tell you how to avoid being financially burdened because of your car. You would be surprised at how much cars are really costing you. Cars are part of American society and are a convenient and necessary mode of transportation for many people, but they can also be a major financial burden. In many ways, cars can take away your freedom and security. Cars can be a financial triple threat. First, let's start with the fact that we borrow money at interest to buy an asset that we have to pay to maintain, and that drastically depreciates in value. A new car can depreciate well over 50 percent in the first five years of owning it, and 10 percent of that will kick in the moment you drive it off the lot. Can you think of anything else you pay so much to buy, keep and maintain that loses value that quickly? Leasing doesn't help with this since they set their prices so that you pay for the vehicle's depreciation, and when it's over and you return it, they still have an asset they can sell. You also have the high cost of insurance, which is required by law in most places, and the cost of coverage can vary widely depending on a number of factors such as the make and model of the car, the age and driving history of the owner, and the location where the car is driven. Most financing companies will require full coverage insurance when you financed the car. Those premiums can be particularly high for drivers considered to be high-risk, such as those with a history of accidents or traffic violations. And when you are 25 years old or less, you are guaranteed to pay higher premiums. So, don't be surprised if you end up having monthly payments well over $600, putting car payments and insurance together. Most people's payments of both together are between $600-$800. Some people pay over $1000 a month to keep their car, and that's not counting maintenance. It can be a lot of money when you are young and going to school. According to Chase bank, the average car payment for a used car as of 2021 was $471.

This is not trashing cars; I am not saying you should not own a car; most people need it to get around. I am just giving you the facts. Now, if you buy a car correctly, you can alleviate the financial burden. If you are not a car person and you only view cars as a tool to get you to places, better for you. When you like cars, you typically tend to spend more. Here are some tips for you to be in the driver's seat and not let your car take you for a ride:

- Buy a car that is at least five years old:

Buying a car that is five years old can help you skip a significant portion of the depreciation that occurs in the first few years of a car's life. When a new vehicle is purchased, it can lose up to 20% of its value in the first year and up to 60% of its value over the first five years. By purchasing a 5-year-old car, you are buying a vehicle that has already undergone this steep depreciation, making you less likely to experience a significant loss in value. At the same time, the car is still pretty new.

In addition to skipping most of the depreciation, a 5-year-old car will likely have lower car payments, as the vehicle will be less expensive to purchase than a brand-new one. Insurance premiums are also typically lower for older cars, as they are considered to be less valuable and therefore less expensive to insure."

Paying for a car in cash can be a smart financial decision, as it allows you to avoid the cost of financing. When you finance a car, you are essentially borrowing money to pay for it, and you will be required to pay interest on the loan. This can significantly increase the overall cost of the car. By contrast, paying for a car in cash allows you to avoid these additional costs and can save you a significant amount of money over time. Now I know that most people won't have the money to buy it in cash, but if it is your first car, you can and should start small. Just try to have as much as possible to put down. You may want to consider saving up and waiting until you have the necessary funds before making a purchase. Don't worry if you don't have thousands of dollars to pay in cash; that's ok. Just if you are going to finance it, try to have as much cash as possible to put down. One of the most important considerations when financing a car is the interest rate, as this will determine how much you will pay for the loan. It is generally a good idea to shop around and compare rates from multiple lenders to ensure that you are getting the best deal possible. Also, putting as much money down as you can will help to reduce the overall cost of the loan and can help to lower your monthly payments.

- If you have good credit, avoid car dealerships:

if you have good credit, that means that you can get financing on your own with your bank of choice. Pick the car you want first and get your own financing from a credit union. Avoid going to the car dealership straight up and have the financing be on their terms. You can use several platforms to buy a used car from private sellers, including Facebook Marketplace, Craigslist, Auto trader CarGurus, Offerup, and cars.com, among others. And many times, people can be more honest than dealerships. Once you have the car you want, either from a person or a dealership, if that's what you want, have your financing already in place from your local credit union. They can either give you a check or cash to pay for the car, and then you just pay the loan that you have with the bank. With this, you avoid a lot of the high-interest fees, doc fees, and many other fees car dealerships will put on you, and you have the loan more on your terms and not on the dealership's terms. Visualize the cost of your car payment and your insurance and make sure to keep it no more than 30% of your income: It is important to carefully consider the cost of your car payment and insurance when determining how much you can afford to spend on a car. A good rule of thumb is to keep these costs no more than 30% of your income, as this will help ensure you do not overburden yourself financially. When calculating the cost of your car payment and insurance, be sure to include any additional expenses such as maintenance, repairs, and fuel. By keeping these costs within a reasonable range, you can avoid financial strain and ensure that you are able to afford the other necessities of life.

When you're looking to buy a car, it's important to make sure it's reliable, so you don't end up with a lemon. Here are some ways to check for reliability:

- Do your research: Look up reviews and ratings of the make and model you're interested in. This will give you an idea of the car's overall reliability and any common issues that have been reported.
- Check for recalls: Check the National Highway Traffic Safety Administration website to see if the car has any open recalls.
- Get a vehicle history report: A vehicle history report will provide information about the car's previous owners, accidents, and any reported issues or repairs.
- Test-drive the car: Take the car for a test drive to get a feel for how it handles and to see if there are any obvious issues. Pay attention to the car's braking, steering, and acceleration.
- Have a mechanic inspect the car: Before making a final decision, have a mechanic inspect the car to check for any potential problems or issues.

Saving And Investing:

Don't worry; I'm not going to get too technical in this section. The last thing I want to do is bore you with specific terms and complicated financing. I just want to give you a simple perspective of both saving and investing so you can understand them and give you ideas about what you can do, molding them depending on your objectives. Saving and investing may sound boring and adult-like, but trust me. Having the basis of this, it's something you'll thank yourself for later on in life.

Saving and investing are two important things that can help you have more money in the future. Saving means putting some of your money in a safe place, like a savings account at a bank. Also, growing your available credit on credit cards by increasing your credit limit or by having a long credit history without using it counts as saving because you have capital available that you can use when needed. Investing means putting your money into something that has the potential to grow in value, like stocks, real estate, a college degree, a side hustle, etc.

When you save money, you're basically keeping it in a place where it's safe and you can get to it easily. You can start by setting aside a small amount of money each week or month and putting it into a savings account. This can be a good way to save up for something you want to buy, whether it's saving for a car, a college education, or a trip.

Investing is a little bit different from saving. Investing means putting your money into something that has the potential to grow in value over time. Like a side hustle or, for example, if you invest in a stock, you're buying a small piece of a company. If the company does well and makes a lot of money, the value of the stock will go up, and you'll make money too. Similarly, if you invest in real estate, you're buying a piece of property, like a house or an apartment. If the value of the property goes up, you'll make money when you sell it. And I know it sounds like you need a lot of money to invest, but your cat start little by little. Also, keep in mind the price and value of every purchase you make. Price is the amount of money you pay for something, while value is how useful or important that thing is to you. For example, a phone may cost a lot of money, but if it has features you need and uses a lot, then it has good value for you. This book's price was pretty low and something that didn't change your wallet, but the value you can get out of it is big. You will always run into things in both ways, things with low prices but high value and things with low value with a high price. Think about both the price and the value of something before you buy it so that you can make smart choices about spending your money.

The key is to start early and be consistent. Saving and investing may not be the most exciting thing, but it's a surefire way to ensure a financially stable future and give you the freedom to do the things you love. So, why not give it a try and see where it takes you?

Here are some examples of investing that don't require a lot of money and that teens can start:

- A side hustle: A side hustle can be a great way to invest your time and money. It's like starting your own mini business on the side of your regular job or school. You put in some time and money to start it up, but if it takes off and becomes successful, it can bring in extra income for you.
- Investing in a Roth IRA, which is a type of retirement account that allows you to invest money on a tax-free basis, and you can start with as little as $50.
- Investing in index funds, which are a type of mutual fund that tracks a stock market index, like the S&P 500. These types of funds are often low-cost and easy to understand.

- Investing in a high-yield savings account, which is a type of savings account that pays a higher interest rate than a traditional savings account. This can help your money grow faster.
- Investing in a micro-investing app, like Acorns or Stash, which allows you to invest small amounts of money and create a diverse portfolio.
- Investing in a cryptocurrency, like Bitcoin, which requires a small amount of money to purchase and can potentially yield high returns.

These are just a few examples to give you an overview of things you can start doing with little money. The thing is to remember that investing doesn't have to be complicated or and to start, you don't require a lot of money. require a lot of money..The key is to start early and be consistent. Saving and investing may not be the most exciting thing, but it's a surefire way to ensure a financially stable future and give you the freedom to do the things you love. So, why not give it a try and see where it takes you?

Good and Bad Debt:

Being in debt is not good for anyone. Debt is the money that you owe and must pay back. You may have borrowed from a lender, such as a bank or credit card company. When you take on debt, you must pay back the money you borrowed, plus interest. However, not all debt is created equal. The concept of good and bad debt refers to the type of debt that you take on. Good debt is debt that is taken on for investments that have the potential to increase in value or generate income. This type of debt is generally considered "worth it" because it can potentially improve your financial situation over the long term.

On the other hand, bad debt is debt that is taken on for purchases that do not have the potential to increase in value or generate income. This type of debt is generally considered "not worth it" because it does not improve your financial situation over the long term. It all depends on how you use the debt and what you plan to get out of it. For example, a student loan may not be bad debt if you use it for a career you are passionate about and will make you money, but it can be if you drop out of college because you realize it was not for you or you did not like the career you chose.

To be mindful of the types of debt you will potentially incur in the future, here are some examples of good and bad debt:

Bad Debt Examples:
Retail store credit card debt:

The most common retail store credit card debts are those incurred through the use of store-branded credit cards, such as the ones offered by department stores, clothing retailers, and electronics stores. These cards typically have high-interest rates and may offer incentives such as discounts or rewards for using the card at a specific store. If you don't manage this properly, the debt from these cards can quickly accumulate and become difficult to pay off.

Some of the most common retail stores that offer store-branded credit cards include:

- Target
- Macy's
- Walmart
- Best Buy
- Home Depot
- Lowe's
- Amazon

- Kohli's
- JCPenney
- Sears

Luxury goods debt: Taking on debt to finance the purchase of luxury goods, such as designer clothing or high-end electronics, is generally considered to be bad debt, terrible debt, actually, because the goods do not have the potential to increase in value. And if you are in debt because of this, you cannot afford it. No need to show off.

Car loans: Taking on a car loan to buy a new car can be considered bad debt because the value of the car typically decreases over time. There are ways a car loan can be considered good debt, but it is typically the exception, not the rule. But you can at least mitigate it by shopping around for the best interest rate, opting for a shorter loan term, choosing a reliable and fuel-efficient car, making extra payments, and using the car for income-generating activities like driving for Uber or Lift, for example. Also, if you never miss a payment, a car can be good to grow your credit. It can be both, but unfortunately, for most people, a car loan ends up being in the "bad debt" category.

Payday loans: Payday loans are terrible. They are high-interest, short-term loans that are designed to be repaid on your next payday. Payday loans are considered bad debt because they typically have very high-interest rates and fees, making it difficult for borrowers to pay them off in a timely manner. Before considering a payday loan, you should avoid them at all costs and explore other options, such as personal loans, credit union loans, or even borrowing from family or friends.

Gambling debt: Gambling debt is taken on to finance gambling activities, such as buying lottery tickets or playing slot machines.

Gambling debt is generally considered bad debt because it is used to fund activities with no inherent value and carries a high risk of loss.

Vacation debt: Taking on debt to finance a vacation is generally considered to be bad debt because the vacation does not have the potential to increase in value or generate income.

Furniture debt: Taking on debt to finance the purchase of furniture is generally considered to be bad debt because the furniture does not have the potential to increase in value.

Wedding debt: Taking on debt to finance a wedding is generally considered to be bad debt because the wedding does not have the potential to increase in value or generate income.

Here at the type of debt that can be good for you:

- Mortgages: A mortgage is a loan used to buy a house. While a mortgage is a significant debt, owning a home can be a good investment because the value of the home may increase over time.
- Small business loans: If you take out a loan to start or expand a small business, the business has the potential to generate income and improve your financial situation.
- Personal loans: Personal loans you use for something that has the potential to make money over time, like investing in a business. That can have the potential to be good debt.
- Credit card debt: there is a trick here, credit card debt can be considered good debt if it is used for things that you would be spending money on anyways, and you are able to pay off the balance in full each month. This can help you build a positive credit history, which can benefit you in the long term when it comes to obtaining loans or credit with

favorable terms. But ONLY if you use them correctly; if not, they are bad debt.

"Good debt" is generally defined as debt that is taken on for investments that have the potential to increase in value or generate income. if these types of debt are not used responsibly, and things do not go according to plan, they can become bad debt and lead to financial problems. The key here and the main point for you to understand is that it all depends on what the debt does for you — and it should always be more than what you do for the debt. The key to managing debt is ensuring that it works for you and not the other way around.

The Importance of Building Credit

MISTAKE#4 Failing To Establish Credit In Your Youth:

Many young people don't know how important it is to start building credit early, or they just don't care. They think, "oh, I'll just miss a payment or two on my first car loan or credit card," but by the time they're 20, their credit score is already in the toilet. Bad credit among young adults is very common. There are a bunch of reasons why young people might not care about credit or not know about it, like not getting educated on it, wanting instant gratification, not having access to credit products, or just being scared of taking on debt.

But here's the thing, having good credit is a big deal. It makes your life easier. You need it to get approved for loans, credit cards, and other financial products, plus landlords and insurance companies might look at your credit score before renting to you or giving you a policy. Some companies check your credit score to hire you. A good credit score can also get you better interest rates and terms on those products, which can save you a ton of money in the long run.

The good news is even if you don't have a steady income or someone to co-sign for you, there are still ways to start building credit early. You can become an authorized user on a parent's credit card, take out a small loan from a credit union, or get a secured credit card. Just make sure to use these products responsibly and pay your bills on time so you can build a solid credit history.

In short, having good credit makes life easier, and if you start working on it while you're young, you'll be ahead of the game because it only takes a few years to have a solid credit score. Meaning by the time you are 25, you can have an 800 credit score. Most 25 years old do not have good credit scores when they could have. Be the exception and have excellent credit in your mid 20s

Most young people either do not care or have a lack of knowledge and just don't start building credit until later in life, maybe in their mid-20s or early 30s. If you start building credit now while you are young, you will have the door open to so many opportunities that most people at that age won't. Building credit at a young age can help you establish a strong financial foundation and set you up for financial success in the future. Many young teens may not have access to credit because they are not old enough to apply for credit cards or loans on their own.

Several options are available for young people trying to build credit. It's important to choose a credit-building strategy that works for you and to use credit responsibly. Here are some ways:

- Get a credit card:

This is very easy. Just get a credit card and start using it. Responsibly, of course. This means paying your bills on time and keeping your credit utilization low, typically below 30%. For example, if you have a credit card with a $500 credit limit, try to avoid using a carry a balance that is too high in that $500 limit. You can get a credit card in different ways, like becoming an authorized user on someone else's credit card, such as a parent or guardian. This can help you build credit as long as the primary cardholder is responsible with their credit. Or you can also get a secured credit card, which is backed by a security deposit that you put in. People with poor or limited credit history often use secured credit cards. Discover is the most popular credit card for this. It works by putting down a small amount, just a few hundred dollars. Then you are essentially using your money as collateral for the credit limit. The deposit you make acts as a guarantee that you'll pay off your debts, and it also determines your credit limit.

In most cases, once you've made your deposit and been approved for the card, you can use it just like a regular credit card to make purchases and withdraw cash. As you make payments, the card issuer will report your activity to the credit bureaus, which can help you build or improve your credit score.

As far as the deposit is concerned, it can be reusable. Once you have established a good payment history and the card issuer is satisfied with your creditworthiness, they may give you the option to increase your credit limit without requiring an additional deposit. If you make your payments on time and in full, it will help to improve your credit score. Late or missed payments, on the other hand, can negatively impact your credit score. Once you have paid off the balance, you can get your deposit back; it all depends on the type of credit card you get.

- Use a credit-builder loan:

A credit-builder loan is a loan specifically designed to help people build credit. These loans typically have a small credit limit and are paid back over a set period of time. Your credit score will improve as you make your loan payments on time.

Have your rent reported to credit bureaus: If you don't know, ask your landlord if they report your rent payment to the credit bureaus. Some landlords may report rent payments to credit bureaus, so paying your rent on time can help you to build credit. If your landlord does not do it, here are a few options:

- Rent reporting services:

There are several third-party companies that specialize in reporting rent payments to credit bureaus. These companies collect your rent payment information from your landlord and report it to the credit bureaus on your behalf.

- Self-Reporting:

Some credit bureaus allow individuals to self-report their rent payments. You will need to provide proof of your rent payments, such as a copy of your lease agreement or rent receipts, using rent tracking apps, for example. There are apps that allow you to track your rent payments, and these apps can report your rent payments to the credit bureaus. These apps are usually free or low-cost.

- Use a credit-reporting service:

Credit-reporting services, such as CreditKarma or Credit Sesame, can help you to build credit by reporting your financial activity to credit bureaus. These services can be a good option for people who have no or very little credit history.

- Get a co-signer:

If you are having trouble getting approved for a credit card or maybe a loan on your own, like a car loan, you may be able to get a co-signer to help you qualify. A co-signer is someone who agrees to take on the responsibility for your debt if you are unable to pay it back. Just be aware that defaulting on your debt could also negatively affect your co-signer's credit.

Why You Should Use Credit Cards for Everything

Credit cards are wonderful tools. If you use them correctly, they will be your best friend. But if you don't use them the right way, they can be your worst enemy. It is like a pit bull; if you train a pitbull the right way, it will defend you, but if you train (in credit card terms, would be "use") the pitbull the wrong way, it can turn against you and attack you. The concept of using credit cards in a way that benefits you is easy, but most people abuse it, and that's why there is so much credit card debt out there. It is better to break down how to use credit cards piece by piece, so here are some tips for using a credit card correctly:

Treat credit cards like debit cards:

Let's say you have a credit card with a $500 limit. You don't have to be spending all of that limit just because you have it. Use a credit card, where you only charge items you would be spending on ANYWAYS, and then use the money you would have spent on that to put it on the credit card. You can start with everyday purchases such as groceries, gas, and bills and pay off the balance each month, or try to get as close as you can. You can demonstrate to the credit bureaus that you can handle credit responsibly, and you can also earn rewards.

Keep your credit utilization low:

In simple terms, your credit utilization is the balance that you have in your credit card compared to your limit. Let's say that you have a credit card with a $1000 limit and a balance of that you owe on the card of $500. That means that your credit utilization is 50%. That means that your credit utilization is 50% since you have a balance of half your credit limit. Typically you want to keep your credit balance below 30%. So that's why I said try to put as much money on that card as you can. That money that you put there you can spend later anyways, so why not do it?

Avoid applying for too many credit cards in a short period of time:

Every time you apply for a credit card, it can result in a hard inquiry on your credit report. You have to know that it hurts your score for a little while. Typically, you only want to apply for 2-3 credit cards per year.

Points, rewards, and sign-up bonuses:

There are different types of credit cards. Many credit card issuers offer rewards programs that allow you to earn points or cash back for your purchases. These rewards can be redeemed for things like merchandise, travel, or statement credits. There are also different types of sign-up bonuses, meaning if you sign up for a credit card, they give you something after spending a certain amount of money, such as cashback or travel rewards. For example, you can achieve an American Express card that offers 75,000 travel points given to you automatically after you spend $1000 dollars on the card, and you have a month to do that. The smart way of taking advantage of something like that is to spend that $1000 on things you would be spending ANYWAY, such as groceries, gas, car payments, and rent, among other things. Find useful things you can spend that money on.

If you use them correctly, credit cards can be a great tool. If you use them incorrectly, they will cost you.

Avoid the following mistakes at all costs:

- Using the full credit limit and making only the minimum payment each month:

This can lead to high-interest charges and make it difficult to pay off the debt. It also can lead to maxing out your credit limit, which can negatively impact your credit score. Do not use the whole limit just because you have it, and pay only the minimum.

- Carrying a balance on multiple cards:

This can lead to high-interest charges and make it difficult to keep track of payments. It's okay to have multiple credit cards because they help with your credit utilization. But try to use just a few of them.

- Making late payments:

This can result in late fees and damage your credit score.

Using credit cards for unnecessary purchases: This comes with being responsible with your money and not buying on impulse. It all depends on your mindset.

If you are smart with your money, you will find credit cards as a great tool to use in your everyday basics. Credit cards can be a useful tool for managing your finances and building credit, but they can also be dangerous if you do not use them responsibly. When used correctly, credit cards can help you earn rewards, build a credit history, and make convenient purchases. However, if you don't have control of your spending habits, credit cards can quickly lead to high levels of debt and financial problems. It's important to understand the terms and conditions of the credit card, set a budget, and track your spending to ensure you use credit cards in a smart and responsible way. According to the latest consumer debt data from the Federal Reserve Bank of New York, in the third quarter of 2022, credit card debt in the United States alone was $925 billion, and you know what? All of that debt is from people who do not use credit cards wisely. The ones who use credit cards the right way are not in that number.

Slow and Steady Wins the Race. Building Wealth Over Time:

So the best way for you to not struggle with money in your future is to take everything that you have learned so far and keep learning more things on your own as well, apply it to your life, and build it up little by little over time. Things happen over time and not overnight. Even if you are not money motivated, you still want to make enough to live a comfortable life and not be stressed about money. Every day counts. Every small action you take brings you one step closer to where you want to be. You have to use a combination of small efforts every day. Every single day can contribute a little bit to your goal. That is how the world works. Patience is also important, as progress may not always be linear, and setbacks may and will occur. It can be helpful to remind yourself of the end goal and the progress that has already been made, so you know that you have made progress again every day. One key to consistently working towards your goals is to create habits and routines that support your progress. This means setting aside dedicated time each day to work towards your goals and making it a regular part of your routine. Building wealth isn't something that happens overnight; it's a slow and steady process. You gotta have patience, put in the work every day, and understand how the money game works. It's important not to get discouraged when things aren't moving as fast as you want. That's just how it goes. Keep track of your progress and set small goals to keep yourself motivated. The earlier you start, the more time your money has to grow. Building wealth over time is a more sustainable and stable approach than trying to make a quick fortune. Money that comes quickly is often just as quickly spent and not invested for long-term growth. You know how it goes; sometimes, people get lucky and hit the jackpot, like winning the lottery or striking it big with crypto or NFTs. But more often than not, that money doesn't stick around for long. It's like the saying goes, "easy come, easy go." Building wealth over time can be done through a variety of routes, both with and without a college education. There's no one right way to do it, so that means that you have to envision the lifestyle you want and find a way to create wealth that would allow that desired lifestyle. Just keep doing the right things over time, and you'll be set.

CHAPTER 3

THE EDUCATION SYSTEM AND YOU

The education system plays a crucial role in shaping your future, particularly as a teenager. As you navigate through your high school years, you will be faced with a multitude of decisions that will ultimately impact your future. One of the most significant decisions you will face is whether to continue your education after high school by going to college. However, this decision is not as simple as it may seem. With the rising cost of tuition and the increasing burden of student loan debt, the decision to go to college is becoming increasingly difficult for many students like you.

The education system is not without its problems; one of the most significant challenges that you may face in the current education system is the high cost of college and how inefficient it can be. One criticism of the current education system is that it is failing to prepare students for the real world. This might be because there's not enough emphasis on practical skills like financial literacy and critical thinking and too much focus on memorizing stuff and taking standardized tests. As you've probably noticed, the education system has its flaws.

In this chapter, we're gonna take a closer look at these issues and how they affect you. We'll talk about the challenges and opportunities you may face in the education system, like the decision to go to college, student debt, and access to quality education. We'll also look at how technology is changing the way we learn and shaping the future of education for students like you.

As you progress through your education, you may have noticed that the system is far from perfect. This chapter will dive deeper into these issues and explore how the education system affects you. We will discuss the challenges and opportunities that you may face in the current education system, including the decision of whether or not to go to college, student debt, and access to quality education. We will also examine the impact of technology on the education system and how it is shaping the future of learning for students like you.

Excitement, Uncertainty, and Confusion:

After high school, it's normal to feel lost or uncertain and like you don't know what the heck you're doing or what you are going to do. It's a big time of change and transition, and it can be overwhelming to think about all the different options and decisions you gotta make. I want you to know that taking your time and exploring your options is okay before making any big decisions. Take some time to figure out what you're into, what you're passionate about, and what's most important to you in life. These are all important questions to consider as you start thinking about what's next.

It's common for teens to feel a mix of emotions like excitement, anxiety, and uncertainty after high school. They may be excited to start a new chapter but also anxious about the unknown and the responsibilities that come with adulthood. Many teens may also feel uncertain about what their next steps should be, whether it be attending college, entering the workforce, or pursuing other opportunities. Research your options and make informed decisions about your future. This can include researching different colleges and their programs, learning about potential career paths, and exploring different forms of education and training. By taking the time to research your options, you can make more informed decisions about your future and set yourself up for success. This chapter has provided guidance to help you navigate this important time in your life, and by following the advice outlined here, you can set yourself up for success as you take the next steps in your journey.

MISTAKE # 5: Going To College Without Knowing What You Want Out Of Life

This is a very common mistake that, unfortunately, many young adults make, they go to college just for the sake of going to college, and they either drop out or end up in a career they didn't really want. This can lead to a lack of direction and purpose in life and also will result in wasted time and money. To avoid this mistake, take the time to explore your interests and values before committing to a college or university program. Many teens are not aware of all the flaws in the college system and the number of opportunities out there to make your desired lifestyle a reality. They don't take into account the debt they will incur, and they don't really know what they want to do, but they jump into a random college program just because their friends are going or their parents pushed them into going. Many of them realize halfway through that the career they chose is not what they really want, and they end up dropping out with the debt they incurred and feeling even more lost in life.

To avoid this, take some time to explore your interests and values before going to college. Get a job in the meantime while you figure it out. Think about what you enjoy doing and what is most important to you in life. Consider your strengths and passions and what you want to achieve in life. These are all important questions to consider as you start thinking about your future. It's also worth figuring out what you want to do first and asking yourself if that requires a college degree. If the answer is no, don't go to college and take time to figure out your next steps on a different path. But don't go just because.

Exposing The Flaws In The Higher Education System:

We all know that education is important, and we're not saying that college is a bad idea. But there are some serious problems with the education system in the United States. The system is supposed to help shape the minds of the next generation, but it's facing a lot of issues that hold people back from reaching their full potential. One of the biggest issues is financial literacy. Many students graduate from high school without a basic understanding of how to manage their money and make good financial decisions. This can make it hard for them to handle the financial challenges of adulthood, like paying rent and bills and not getting into a lot of debt. Entrepreneurship is another area where the school system doesn't prepare students well enough. While some schools may offer business or economics classes, they don't teach students how to start and run their own businesses or find opportunities in the market to make a living doing what they want.

The school system also doesn't always teach students essential life skills like time management, effective communication, self-awareness, problem-solving, and critical thinking. These skills are crucial for success in any career, yet they are not always emphasized in the classroom. The education system is also slow to adapt to new teaching methods. Many schools and universities still use traditional teaching methods that focus on rote learning and memorization. This approach doesn't work well in the modern world and doesn't prepare students for the challenges they'll face in the real world.

Loneliness is a big problem in college too. The education system doesn't put enough emphasis on mental health and well-being. With the pressure to excel academically, many students struggle with anxiety, depression, and other mental health issues, but schools often don't have the resources or support to help them. This can make students feel overwhelmed and stressed, which is a major problem and a public health concern.

Another issue to watch out for is college debt. The rising cost of college tuition makes it hard for many students and families to afford a college education, which can lead to students taking on large amounts of student loan debt. According to the Federal Reserve, the total amount of student loan debt in the United States is over $1.7 trillion. This can have a lot of negative consequences for young people and the economy, like limiting consumer spending, hindering savings and investment, stifling innovation and entrepreneurship, and limiting labor market mobility. This can have a ripple effect on the economy and restrict economic growth and job creation. The high cost of college and the burden of student loan debt makes college education less accessible, particularly for students from low-income backgrounds. This can perpetuate cycles of poverty and limit opportunities for these students. Additionally, many students are not finding employment after graduation, which can be due to a mismatch between the skills taught in college and the job market's needs or a lack of job opportunities in specific fields.

Paying for a kid's college education can be a real pain for families, especially if they're already struggling to make ends meet. Low-income families or those who didn't save enough for their child's education can have an especially hard time. Even if you decide to go to college, you may find that you're not as interested in your classes or having trouble keeping up with the workload and end up dropping out. But even if you don't complete your degree, you'll still be left with student loan debt which can be a real bummer for your finances. You may not be able to afford big purchases, like a house or a car, and saving for retirement can be a challenge. It can also make it harder to start your own business or take risks in your career, which can limit how much money you can make. And if you want to keep learning and growing your skills, it can make that harder too. And on top of all that, it can mess with your credit score, making it harder for you to borrow money in the future. So, college debt can be a real pain for a person's finances, so you want to avoid that if possible.

Pursuing College or a Different Route:

When it comes to going to college, you have to make a decision based on your own interests and goals. A college degree it's not the right choice for everyone. Consider the financial burden of student loan debt before making a decision. Do not see it from the perspective of going to college just because. Ask yourself what you want to be doing in the next 5-10 years, and does that require a college degree? If the answer is yes, then you should go to college because you need it to achieve that. Here are some examples of typical careers that require a degree:

- Lawyer
- Doctor
- Engineer
- Teacher
- Nurse
- Dentist

- Optometrist
- Veterinarian
- Physical Therapist
- Occupational Therapist
- Speech Therapist
- Accountant

So, of course, if you decide that you want to follow a career of this nature, of course, you should go to college, just make sure the degree you choose is worth the debt.

If you are unsure whether or not you should go to college, DO NOT GO, at least until you figure it out. Going to college without a clear sense of what you want to do is not a wise decision. College is a significant investment of time and money, so it's important to clearly understand what you want to achieve and how college can help you get there. If you're unsure, it may be a sign that you're not passionate about a specific career and are just looking to make a living. College is not the only path to a successful career and a good income. There are many different options for education and training, such as trade schools, apprenticeships, or online programs, that can provide the specific skills needed for certain careers. Also, some careers, such as entrepreneurship or self-employment, do not require a college degree. Many online and offline business opportunities are available, depending on your skills, interests, and resources. In today's world, there are many opportunities to make a living doing what you love, thanks to the internet. With the vast array of online platforms and tools available, it's possible to turn your passions and skills into a successful career. From starting an e-commerce business to becoming a freelance writer or designer to creating content on social media, the internet has opened up a world of possibilities for people to make a living doing what they enjoy. It's important to research and explore the options available and to be willing to put in the work and effort to make it a success. Starting a business takes time, effort, and resources and is not always easy. If you take something from this section, follow your desired lifestyle, analyze your situation before making any big moves, and do not go to college if you are unsure about your future. Only go if your desired career needs a degree.

If you decide to go to College:

When considering going to college, weigh the potential benefits of a college education against the cost. Choosing to pursue a college degree is a significant decision that can have a long-lasting impact on an individual's career and financial future. With the rising cost of tuition and the increasing burden of student loan debt, carefully consider whether a college degree is worth the investment.To make sure that the degree you get is worth the debt you take on, you can do the following:

- Research the job market: Before you commit to a college or program, research the job market for the career you want to pursue. Look for information about the average salary for the field, the job outlook, and the level of competition for jobs. This will help you understand whether the investment in your education is likely to pay off in the long run.
- Look for scholarships and grants: Look for scholarships, grants, and other financial aid that can help you pay for college without having to take on as much debt. Some scholarships are based on merit, while others are based on need.
- Consider alternative options: Consider alternative options like trade schools, apprenticeships, or online programs. These options can often be more affordable and may

provide the specific skills you need for the career you want to pursue.

- Compare costs: Compare the costs of different colleges and programs to find the most affordable option. Look at the total cost of attendance, including tuition, room and board, and other fees.
- Graduating on time: Make a plan to graduate on time, as every extra year of college, you take on additional debt, so it's important to keep that in mind and plan accordingly.
- Consider your future: Consider the future potential of the career you are planning on pursuing. You may want to think about the career's growth potential, job stability, and earning potential.

It's a big decision, and you gotta consider all these things before you make your move. Do some research on the job market and the average salary for different degrees and fields so you can get an idea if the cost of your degree is worth it in the long run. Also, check out the job outlook and chances of finding a job in your desired field so you know your future prospects.

Another thing to think about is the type of college you wanna go to. Public colleges may be cheaper than private ones but may not have as many resources and opportunities. So weigh the pros and cons and explore all options for financial aid, scholarships, and grants to help reduce the cost of your degree.

Also, don't sleep on alternative forms of education and training. Trade schools, apprenticeships, or online programs can give you the specific skills you need for certain careers and may be more cost-effective than a traditional college degree.

Just remember to have realistic expectations about the job market and earning potential for different careers, and have a plan to pay off any debt. It'll take a long time and a lot of effort to pay off a lot of debt, so seek help from a financial advisor or counselor to help you navigate the financial aspect of college and find the best option for you.

Overall, it's a big decision, so make sure you have a clear idea of what you want to achieve and how a college degree can help you get there.

Avoiding As much Unnecessary Debt As Possible:

Going to college and avoiding debt is not an easy task. It depends highly on the career you choose. Some careers are much more affordable than others. I will name a few things you can do to avoid or minimize that debt.

Choose an affordable school: Consider the cost of tuition and fees and the availability of financial aid. Look for schools offering generous financial aid packages or a strong track record of helping students graduate with minimal debt.

Take on a part-time job: Consider working part-time to help cover your expenses. This can also provide valuable experience and help you build skills that can be useful in your future career.

Be mindful of your spending: Try to live frugally while in college. Minimize unnecessary expenses and avoid overspending.

Explore all your financial aid options: Filling out the Free Application for Federal Student Aid (FAFSA) is the first step in applying for financial aid. Look into grants, scholarships, and work-study programs, as these do not have to be repaid. There are several different types of loans available for college students, including

1. Federal student loans: These loans are provided by the government and include Direct Subsidized Loans, Direct Unsubsidized Loans, and Direct PLUS Loans.

2. Private student loans: These loans are provided by private lenders and typically have higher interest rates than federal student loans.
3. Parent PLUS loans: These loans are available to parents of dependent undergraduate students and are based on the creditworthiness of the parent borrower.
4. Consolidation loans: These loans allow borrowers to combine multiple federal student loans into one loan with a single monthly payment.
5. State-sponsored student loans: Some states also offer student loan programs to their residents.

If you're not ready to jump into college right away, consider taking a gap year and working to save up some money before starting college. If you can find a way to combine your passion with other ways to make money, even better. Also, if you do have to take out loans, make sure you understand the terms and conditions, including the interest rate and repayment terms you will have. Only borrow what you need and try to minimize the amount of debt you take on.

Remember, you cannot get rid of student loan debt through bankruptcy. It's seen as an investment in your future earning potential and ability to repay the loan. And with the rising cost of college tuition, it's becoming harder for some people to afford a college education, leading to an increase in student loan debt. So, make sure you plan and make wise choices.

If You Decide NOT To Go To College:

First, I want to tell you this: If you decide not to go to college, it is not a bad decision. Please don't feel like you're making a mistake or feel bad about it. College is not the only path to success; there are many other ways to acquire the knowledge and skills needed to pursue your desired lifestyle. Some individuals may enter the workforce immediately after high school, while others may follow vocational or technical training. Some may opt to start their own business or learn through self-education.

Take some time for yourself and research what you can do. If you decided no to go is probably because you do not feel attracted to a specific career that requires a degree, and that is totally ok. In life, you will be either in action mode or research mode. Meaning you are in the process of figuring things out or taking action, sometimes both. After high school, I recommend you be in research mode before you decide to move on with anything.

A gap year can be an excellent way to explore different interests and career options before committing to a particular path. This extra time can also be used to research careers and businesses you want to do, shadow professionals, and gain experience in your field of interest.

The transition to adulthood can be exciting and overwhelming for high school graduates. On one hand, you have the freedom to make your own choices and start your own path in whatever way you like, but on the other hand, you may be uncertain about what that path should be. If you're unsure about what to do after high school, keep in mind that it is totally normal and happens to most people of your age. Many people go through this same experience; with time and patience, you can figure out your next move.

This will take some time, but that is much better than going to college without knowing, getting into debt, and then figuring out that it is different from what you wanted to do.

Also, do not think that you will not be educated if you do not go to college. Regarding education, you don't have to commit to a four-year degree. Education is not limited to attending college. Many successful individuals did not attend college or drop out.

There are many other ways to gain knowledge and skills, such as online courses, apprenticeships, on-the-job training, self-study, workshops, etc. College is just one option for education. Get a good-paying job where you can make enough to support yourself and research. YouTube is an excellent tool for learning about business opportunities, careers, life paths, and overall finding yourself. It offers a wide variety of educational videos and content. Many channels provide information and insights on various industries and professions, as well as tutorials and tips on skills and techniques related to those fields. Many businesses and entrepreneurs also use YouTube to promote their products and services and share their experiences and insights.

Here are some different search terms you can use on YouTube to help you find your purpose and figure out what to do after high school if you are unsure:

"Life after high school"
"Discovering your purpose after high school."
"Making decisions after high school"
"Career self-discovery for young adults"
"Navigating life after high school"
"Exploring your options after high school"
"Finding your path in life"
"Discovering your career passions."
"Finding your calling after high school".
Is college worth it?"
"Alternatives to college"
"Pros and cons of college"

Remember that the path to success is rarely straightforward and often involves detours, but never lose sight of your dreams and values. With hard work, perseverance, and a growth mindset, you have the power to create the life you want and achieve your goals. Believe in yourself and trust the journey; each step you take and each challenge you face will bring you one step closer to realizing your full potential. So keep pushing forward, stay true to who you are, and never give up on your aspirations. You've got this!

CHAPTER 4

SCHOOL, FRIENDSHIPS, AND RELATIONSHIPS

It is not uncommon for teenagers to struggle socially and feel lonely at times. In today's world, many factors contribute to social isolation and loneliness among teenagers. Adolescence can be difficult, as young people are trying to figure out who they are and where they fit in.

One common reason that teenagers may struggle with friendships is that they are going through many changes. They may feel different from their peers and have difficulty relating to them. They may also be more self-conscious and sensitive to rejection, making it difficult to create and maintain friendships. Unfortunately, feeling lonely can be a normal part of adolescence. Even if a teenager has a group of friends, they may still feel lonely if they don't feel truly connected. Since it is common for teens to struggle with social skills, making friends, and building a social circle, many teens may feel unsure of themselves and their place in the social world. The increased use of technology and social media makes it more difficult for teens to learn and practice critical social skills. Still, with time, guidance, and support, many teens can develop and improve their social skills and build positive relationships with people.

Social media platforms like Facebook, Instagram, and TikTok make it easy for teens to connect with people. Still, these connections are often superficial and need more depth and intimacy of face-to-face interactions. Additionally, social media can pressure teens to present a curated version of themselves, making them feel inadequate or left out if they don't measure up to their peers.

You're not alone if you're feeling lonely and struggling with social skills. Many people experience social challenges at different points in their lives, and improving social skills with practice is possible. So don't be discouraged, and remember that everyone goes through tough times, but with time, effort, and support, you can develop the social skills you need to build a successful and fulfilling social circle.

MISTAKE #6 Not Understanding You Need To Invest In Yourself

Let me be clear: Many of these mistakes are not entirely your fault, and the school system is to blame for not teaching this and not giving you proper guidance. You need to know this: you must always be investing in yourself. Investing in yourself means taking the time and effort to improve yourself, whether it be physically, mentally, emotionally, or financially. It can include things like working out, learning new skills, and activities such as reading, watching or listening to something that can inspire or educate you. This type of self-improvement can lead to "aha" moments, where you gain new insights or perspectives that can help you better understand yourself and the world around you. By continuously improving yourself, you gain the skills, knowledge, and resilience necessary to tackle any obstacle that comes your way, as well as become more confident, self-assured, and capable of achieving your goals. The goal is to make yourself a better, more well-rounded person. Right now, you are reading or listening to this book, so you are indeed investing in yourself. So, congratulations on that!

Becoming the best version of yourself is always the goal. If you make yourself a lifelong learner, you will prosper, and overcoming anything that comes your way will be easier. If you don't, life will be harder for you, and you will be less prepared and prone to making more mistakes.

Know Your Identity With These Questions:

- What is important to you?
- What do you stand for?
- What do you believe in?
- What are your long-term goals and aspirations?
- What are your strengths and weaknesses?
- Are you introverted or extroverted?
- Are you more of a logical thinker, or do you go more by your emotions?
- What do you love to do?
- What are you naturally drawn to?
- Who are the people you surround yourself with? Or are you alone most of the time?
- How do you want to grow and evolve as a person in the future
- What do you need in order to feel fulfilled and satisfied in life?
- What do your relationships say about you?

- What have you learned from your experiences?
- What has shaped the person you are today?
- What do you enjoy doing, and what are your passions?
- How do you handle stress and difficult situations?
- What are your priorities in life?
- is there something you are trying to achieve?
- How do you define success?
- What are your core beliefs, and how do they influence your worldview?

Being yourself is a continuous process of finding and being who you become over and over again. You improve, you are a different person, and you are that person. As we go through life, we constantly learn and grow, which can cause us to change and evolve as individuals. Being yourself also means accepting yourself as you are, flaws and all. It's about being comfortable in your own skin and not trying to fit into someone else's expectations or ideas of who you should be. It's about being true to who you are, even if that means being different from others. It is completely okay to be different from others. Everyone is unique and has their own individual strengths, weaknesses, perspectives, and experiences. Embracing one's individuality and differences is important for personal growth and self-acceptance.

At the same time, it's also important to acknowledge that there is always room for improvement. We all have areas in our lives where we can grow and develop. The key is to find a balance between accepting ourselves as we are and striving to become the best versions of ourselves. It's not about trying to change who we are but rather about becoming more self-aware and working on the areas where we want and need to improve. This way, we can find fulfillment and satisfaction while being true to ourselves. There is no need to be someone who we are not. In fact, trying to be someone else can lead to feelings of inadequacy and dissatisfaction. Everyone has their own unique qualities and characteristics, and it is important to accept and embrace who we are. When we are true to ourselves, we are more authentic and genuine in our interactions with others, which will lead to stronger and more meaningful relationships. Social skills are not something that you are either born with or not born with. Instead, they are a set of abilities that can be learned and developed over time through practice and experience. Just like any other skill, social skills can be improved with practice, effort, and dedication. Of course, some people may have a natural talent for socializing and making connections with others more than you do, but this does not mean that you cannot develop these skills. With time, effort, and practice, anyone can become more confident and effective in social situations. So, don't be discouraged if you feel that you struggle with social skills. You can learn and improve.

Social Skills in a Digital Age:

In today's digital age, everyone, including teens and young adults, faces many challenges when it comes to developing social skills. One of the biggest challenges is the proliferation of social media and other online platforms, which can make it easier for teens to connect with others, but also make it more difficult for them to develop the face-to-face communication skills that are so important in building and maintaining relationships.

When people feel uncomfortable in social situations, they may retreat and avoid them, which can lead to a vicious cycle of decreased social interaction and worsening social skills.

Social media has greatly changed the way we communicate and connect with others. On the one hand, it has made it easier to stay in touch with friends and family and has given people the ability to connect with others who share similar interests, regardless of where they are located. It has also allowed for the sharing of information and ideas on a global scale, which can be beneficial for personal and professional growth.

On the other hand, social media can also have negative effects on individuals and society as a whole. It has been linked to increased feelings of loneliness, depression, and anxiety, as well as the spread of misinformation. It can also create unrealistic expectations and comparisons, leading to low self-esteem and self-worth. Social media can also be addictive and can consume a lot of time and attention, taking away from real-life interactions and activities.

Your Competence Will Become Your Confidence

As you develop and improve your skills, abilities, and knowledge in a particular area, your level of confidence in your ability to perform will also increase. Meaning that if you don't feel confident about your social skills is because you are not that competent in that area just yet. In other words, as you become more competent in a particular task or activity, you will gain confidence in your ability to do it successfully. It's like, if you're learning a new language, at first, you might feel unsure about your ability to speak it. But as you keep practicing and getting better, your confidence in speaking the language will grow too. The same happens with social skills or any other skill you want to improve. Practice really does make perfect.

The more you practice talking to people, initiating and flowing with conversations, the better you'll become at it.

By putting yourself in social situations and actively engaging with others, you can build your confidence and develop your ability to communicate effectively.

As a teen, there are several different aspects to consider when it comes to developing your social skills. Here are some key areas to focus on:

- Communication skills: This includes your ability to communicate effectively with others, including speaking clearly, making eye contact, and using appropriate body language.
- Active listening: This involves really paying attention to what others are saying, showing interest in their perspectives, and asking questions to clarify their thoughts and feelings.
- Conflict resolution: Being able to effectively handle conflicts and disagreements with others is a valuable social skill to have. This includes learning how to communicate your needs, listen to others, and find mutually acceptable solutions.
- Empathy: This involves the ability to understand and share the feelings of others. By being empathetic, you can build stronger relationships and better understand the perspectives of others.
- Emotional intelligence: This involves understanding and managing your own emotions and being able to recognize and respond to the emotions of others.
- Assertiveness: This involves being able to clearly communicate your needs, boundaries, and opinions while also respecting the rights of others.

- Networking: This involves building and maintaining relationships with others, including making new connections and nurturing existing ones.

Improving your social skills is something you'll be doing for the rest of your life. It's not like you can just learn it all and be done with it. As you grow and change, your social skills may need to change too. And as you meet new people and have new experiences, you'll have the chance to keep learning and getting better.

Social Skills In High School. Building And Maintaining Relationships

You're not alone if you find yourself with few friends in high school or college, and it's difficult for you to maintain a social circle. Making and keeping friends in high school is challenging for everyone. It's not just you; it's the whole environment. High school has its own set of pressures and social dynamics that make it difficult for teenagers to form close relationships. Being a teenager is already tough, with all the changes and growth happening, and high school can add to that with its competitiveness and stress, which makes it even harder to open up and trust others.

On top of that, peer pressure and the desire to fit in with certain groups can make forming real connections even harder. So, it's more than you who is facing these challenges. This is a common problem that almost everyone faces.

Recognizing the difficulties of making and keeping friends in high school is an essential first step in improving your social situation. Understanding high school's unique social dynamics and pressures can help you navigate them more effectively. Once you're aware of the challenges, you can start to develop strategies to overcome them, such as improving your communication skills, building self-confidence, and learning how to deal with rejection and disappointment. Developing social skills and becoming more comfortable interacting with others takes time and practice. If you're not naturally outgoing or socially confident, developing these skills may take more effort and practice. Remember that everyone starts from a different place. Be patient with yourself and remember that social skills are like any other skill, and take time and practice to improve.

A key strategy is to improve your communication skills. Effective communication is crucial for building and maintaining friendships, and this means learning how to listen and express yourself effectively, as well as understanding and interpreting nonverbal cues.

Social media has also contributed to loneliness and isolation, especially in school and college settings where face-to-face interactions are essential for building and maintaining relationships.

Here are some tips and tricks to improve your social situation in school or college

- Take the time to learn about social skills: Taking the time to improve your social skills can definitely help you feel better in social situations. It's like learning anything else, it takes time and practice, but it's worth it in the end. Working on your social skills, like communication, listening, and understanding body language, can make you feel more confident and comfortable around other people. And don't forget about building self-confidence, dealing with rejection, and handling stress in social situations. Just remember, everyone starts from a different place, so don't beat yourself up if you don't see results right away. But with time and effort, you'll definitely see improvements in your social life.

- Smile and make eye contact: When you meet someone new, smiling and making eye contact can help you seem approachable and friendly. This makes it easier for others to approach you and start a conversation.

- Join clubs and activities: Joining clubs or extracurricular activities that interest you is a great way to meet people who share similar passions and hobbies. You can bond over shared interests and have a natural starting

- Introduce yourself: Don't be afraid to take the initiative and introduce yourself to new people. This can be especially helpful when starting a new school or joining a new class. Introducing yourself can break the ice and start building relationships from the beginning.

- Show interest in others: When you meet someone new, ask them about themselves and show a genuine interest in what they have to say. People are more likely to want to be friends with someone who takes the time to listen and learn about them.

- Make plans: If you want to get to know someone better, take the initiative to make plans to hang out. Whether it's a lunch date, a movie night, or a study session, spending time together can help build a stronger relationship.

- Be a good listener: Being a good listener is a key aspect of making friends. When someone is speaking, pay attention and try to understand their perspective. This shows that you value their thoughts and opinions and can help build trust and rapport.

- Be yourself: Don't try to be someone you're not to impress others. Being authentic will attract people who appreciate and accept you for who you are.

- Find common ground: Look for things you have in common with others and use that as a starting point for conversation. Whether it's a shared interest, hobby, or background, finding common ground can help you connect with others and build relationships.
- Don't be afraid of rejection: Not everyone will be interested in being friends with you, and that's okay. Don't take rejection personally, and keep trying with others. Building friendships takes time and effort, and rejection is a normal part of the process.
- Be persistent: Building friendships takes time and effort, so don't give up if you don't make a friend right away. Keep putting yourself out there, join clubs and activities, and reach out to others. Eventually, you'll find the right people who you can build strong and lasting relationships with.

The best tips to get people to like you and talk to you:

- Make it more about them and less about you: A good book about this is "How To Win Friends And Influence People." Making the conversation about the other person, showing genuine interest in them, and getting them to talk about themselves is one of the best ways to get people to talk to you and be interested in you. When you show interest in others, they will show interest in you. By asking people about their interests, hobbies, and experiences, you not only get to know them better, but you also make them feel valued and appreciated. People are naturally drawn to individuals who show interest in them and make them feel heard and understood. By making the conversation about the other person, you can build rapport and establish a foundation for a strong and meaningful relationship.

70

- Use flattery and praise: Using flattery and praising others is a great way to get people to like you because they feel valued and appreciated. When you compliment a person, you make them like you immediately because we like people who like us. Try this and compliment someone, and you will see the way they look at you. By focusing on the positive aspects of the situation and recognizing the achievements of others, you can build a more positive and supportive relationship.

- Remember and call people by their name: A person's name is the sweetest and most important sound in any language to that person. Using someone's name in conversation can personalize the interaction and make them feel valued and remembered. This can help to build rapport and establish a more relaxed and enjoyable atmosphere, leading to a stronger relationship. Remembering someone's name and using it in conversation shows that you value them and pay attention to their interests and experiences, helping to build trust and establish a foundation for a strong and meaningful relationship.

- Be likable: Likeability refers to the extent to which someone is perceived as friendly, approachable, and positive by others. Being likable is one of the most important aspects of social skills and communication because it greatly impacts how others perceive and interact with you. People are naturally drawn to likable individuals and are more likely to want to form relationships with those who are friendly, approachable, and positive. When people feel good around you and enjoy being in your presence, they are more likely to trust you, support you, and be willing to engage in meaningful and productive conversations with you. In addition, being likable can improve your communication skills and make it easier to influence others in a positive way. When people feel comfortable and relaxed around you, they are more likely to be receptive to your ideas and suggestions and open to working with you on common goals and objectives.

Behaviors To Avoid That Could Make You Look Weird Or Awkward:

- Sharing too much, too soon about yourself: Sharing too much personal information too soon can be a common mistake in social interactions. When people share intimate details about their lives, thoughts, and feelings before others are ready to hear them, it can make the other person feel overwhelmed or uncomfortable. This can be especially true when the information is negative or sensitive in nature. Over-sharing can also give others the impression that you are not trustworthy or that you are not good at maintaining boundaries. This can make it difficult for others to feel comfortable around you and can damage the potential for building strong relationships. It's important to be mindful of the information you share and to build trust gradually over time. This means being selective about what you share and only sharing information when it is appropriate and necessary. Doing so can establish a positive reputation and build strong relationships based on mutual trust and respect.
- Lack of filter: Speaking without a filter can be off-putting to others and can cause harm to social interactions and relationships. Suppose you are prone to saying taboo things, using profanity in inappropriate situations, or discussing touchy subjects such as religion and politics without considering relevance or appropriateness. In that

case, you may struggle in your social life. It's important to be mindful of others and to think before speaking. Consider the setting, the people you're speaking to, and their potential reactions to what you're saying. By using good judgment and avoiding saying things that are likely to cause harm, you can maintain positive relationships and avoid social awkwardness.

- Beware of the way you enter and exit a conversation: The way you enter and exit a conversation can also impact your social interactions. Interrupting others, not listening actively, or abruptly leaving a conversation can make you seem rude or disinterested. It's important to be mindful of these things and make an effort to enter and exit conversations in a polite and appropriate manner.

- Lacking relevance: Keeping a conversation relevant and on topic is important for effective communication. When a conversation strays from the subject at hand, it can become confusing and disjointed, and people may lose interest. Staying focused on the topic and making an effort to contribute to the conversation in a meaningful way can help you connect with others and build stronger relationships. Additionally, showing interest in what others have to say and actively listening to their perspective can help keep the conversation relevant and engaging for everyone involved.

- Not enough or too much physical distance when talking: Maintaining the appropriate physical distance when talking to someone is crucial for nonverbal communication. Standing too close to someone can make them feel uncomfortable while standing too far away can make you seem distant or uninterested. It's important to be mindful of personal space and to respect the boundaries of others. In general, maintaining a comfortable distance of about two to four feet is a good rule of thumb for most social situations. In addition to physical distance, maintaining appropriate eye contact is also important. Too much eye contact can be perceived as intense or threatening, while too little eye contact can make you seem disinterested or untrustworthy. Finding a balance between the two can help you build trust and establish a positive connection with others.

- Being overly talkative: If you're always talking, cutting people off, or dominating the convo, it can make you come across as too much to handle and hard to be around. When someone is overly talkative, they tend to dominate conversations and leave little room for others to contribute. This behavior can be perceived as selfish or inconsiderate and can make people feel unheard or unvalued. Additionally, constantly talking without taking a break to listen to others can make you seem self-absorbed and not interested in what others have to say. This can be especially problematic in social situations where the goal is to build relationships and connect with others. People are less likely to want to engage in further interactions with someone who seems overwhelming or difficult to be around. In order to build positive relationships and avoid social awkwardness, it's important to be mindful of how much you're talking and to allow others to contribute to the conversation as well

- Being too quiet: On the other hand, being too shy or not speaking up during a conversation can give off the vibe that you're not interested or unfriendly. When you don't participate in a conversation or share your thoughts and opinions, it can make others feel like you're not interested in them or the conversation. This can lead to an awkward and uncomfortable atmosphere, making it difficult to build relationships with others

- Inappropriate body language: Uncomfortable posture, fidgeting, and avoiding eye contact can make someone seem nervous or uncomfortable, which can come across as weird or awkward.

- Inappropriate humor: Using humor is a great way to lighten the mood and connect with others, but make sure that your jokes are appropriate and in good taste. Jokes that are off-topic, insensitive, or that cross the line can have the opposite effect and make you seem weird insensitive or just akward. This can damage your social interactions and relationships, and make others feel uncomfortable around you or offended. Consider the context, the people you're speaking to, and their potential reactions to what you're saying. Avoid making jokes about sensitive topics like religion, politics, or race, and avoid using humor that could be considered offensive or hurtful. By using humor in an appropriate and considerate way, you can improve your social interactions and make others feel more comfortable and relaxed around you

- Being too personal: When it comes to social interactions, it's important to be mindful of the information you share and the questions you ask. Being too personal or asking personal questions too soon can make the other person feel uncomfortable and even violated. It's important to build trust gradually and only share information when it is appropriate and necessary. Similarly, it's important to respect the boundaries of others and not ask questions that are too personal or intimate. This can include things like asking about someone's salary, relationship status, or other sensitive topics. By being mindful of what you share and what you ask.

- Being overly nervous: Being nervous in a social setting can definitely be a confidence killer, making you come across as weird or uncomfortable to others. This can be especially true if you're sweating profusely, stammering over your words, or fidgeting constantly. These physical cues can make it seem like you're not in control of the situation or that you're feeling anxious, which can make others feel uncomfortable around you. In social situations, people tend to look for cues that signal confidence and relaxation, so appearing nervous can be a major red flag. It can make people feel like they need to avoid you or that they're not going to have a good time around you. If you're someone who struggles with

- Having poor hygiene: Neglecting personal grooming can definitely have a negative impact on your social interactions. When you don't take care of your hygiene, it sends the message that you don't care about yourself or the people you're interacting with. This can make you seem unkempt, unprofessional, and even unapproachable. Simple things like brushing your teeth, showering regularly, and keeping your hair clean and style can go a long way in making you look and feel more presentable. Body odor is another important aspect of personal grooming that can make or break your social interactions. Using deodorant, washing your clothes regularly, and practicing good hygiene habits can help you avoid body odor and maintain a clean and fresh scent. By paying attention to these small details, you can make a good impression and increase your likability in social situations.

We're not saying you gotta be a stickler for political correctness 24/7 and let people boss you around. It's just about being conscious of social norms and how your words and actions affect others. Socializing is a two-way street, so it's crucial to be thoughtful of others if you want to build solid relationships. This doesn't mean you gotta walk on eggshells or constantly worry about what others think, but it does mean being aware of social norms and putting in the effort to be considerate and relevant in your interactions. By being mindful of these things, you can steer clear of awkward or uncomfortable social situations and strengthen your relationships. Sure, you can ignore social norms, but you can't ignore the consequences, like making others feel uneasy, offending them, or ruining relationships. While it's important to stay true to yourself and not let societal norms dictate your actions, it's also important to be mindful of how your behavior affects others. By being conscious of social norms and thinking about their impact, you can foster positive relationships and avoid unintended consequences

Emotional Intelligence And Self-Awareness:

Emotional intelligence is all about understanding and managing your own emotions. It is basically like being in control of your feelings. Imagine being able to stay cool when you're angry or pumped up when you're excited instead of just lashing out or losing focus. It's also about understanding how other people are feeling and being able to communicate with them effectively.

Having emotional intelligence can make a huge difference in your life. It can make your relationships stronger, help you do better in school or work, and just make you feel better overall. And the good news is, it's a skill you can work on and get better. Another part of emotional intelligence is being self-aware, which means paying attention to your own thoughts and feelings and how they influence your behavior. By doing this, you can make better decisions, communicate better with others, and have fewer conflicts in your relationships. Emotional intelligence is an important skill that can be developed and practiced over time. By being self-aware of our emotions and how they impact our thoughts and behaviors, as well as being sensitive to the emotions of others, we can improve our relationships, work performance, and overall well-being.

The way you practice emotional intelligence is by becoming more aware of and in control of your own emotions, as well as being better at understanding and relating to the emotions of others. Here are some ways to work on it:

Self-reflection: Take some time each day to think about how you're feeling, what you're thinking, and how you're behaving. This will help you understand yourself better.

Emotional regulation: When things get tough, try to stay calm and in control of your emotions. You can do this by taking deep breaths, counting to 10, or finding a healthy outlet for your emotions, such as exercise or journaling.

Mindfulness: Do things like meditate or do yoga to help you stay focused on the present moment and aware of your emotions.

Empathy: Try to see things from other people's perspectives and understand how they're feeling. You can do this by listening closely, asking questions, and trying to imagine what they're going through.

Communication skills: Work on your communication skills, such as active listening, speaking clearly and appropriately, and resolving conflicts effectively.

Feedback: Ask friends, family, or coworkers for honest feedback on your emotional intelligence. This will help you see what you're doing well and what you need to work on.

Why You Shouldn't Compare Yourself to Others: Embrace Your Unique Path

It's all too easy to compare ourselves to others when we're constantly scrolling through social media. Platforms like Facebook, Instagram,

TikTok, and Snapchat often show a highly curated version of people's lives, highlighting only the positive aspects and best moments. This can create a distorted view of reality, making it seem like everyone else has it all figured out while our own lives appear less perfect by comparison. Keep in mind that what we see on social media is not always an accurate representation of the truth. People tend to present a selective version of themselves and their lives, and it can be easy to forget that behind the photos and videos, everyone has their own struggles, insecurities, and problems.

Comparing ourselves to others on social media can bring about feelings of jealousy, frustration, and disappointment, which can have negative effects on our mental health and overall well-being. Remember that everyone's journey is unique and different, shaped by their own set of experiences, challenges, and opportunities. Comparing ourselves to others is not only unfair, but it's also unproductive, as it takes our focus away from our own goals and progress.

Instead of comparing ourselves to others, it's better to focus on our own journey and progress. This means setting and achieving our own goals, working towards becoming the best version of ourselves, and recognizing our own strengths and weaknesses. It also means being grateful for the opportunities and challenges that come our way rather than feeling inadequate or frustrated. Our journey is unique, and we shouldn't waste our time comparing ourselves to others. By focusing on our own growth and development, we can maintain a positive outlook and improve our mental health and well-being. Do not compare your chapter 1 with someone else chapter 7.

Beyond the Opinion of Others: It doesn't matter what people think of you

This section may sound contradictory to you because we have been talking about social norms and following them, so we don't appear weird or awkward so we can have a good social life. But at the same time, you have to find the balance between building positive relationships and maintaining your individuality and persona. It's totally normal to want to be liked and accepted by your friends, crush, or even your parents. But it's easy to get caught up in caring too much about what others think of you and let that hold you back with everything. Stop caring so much of what other people think; at the end of the day, people's opinions of you really don't matter that much in the big picture. Everyone's different, and it's impossible to please everyone all the time.

People's opinions are just that - opinions. They're based on their own thoughts and perceptions and don't always reflect reality, and most importantly, rarely affect YOUR reality. Just because someone has a certain opinion of you doesn't mean it's true or should affect how you feel about yourself. People have their own biases, prejudices, and perspectives, and their opinions of you might be influenced by their own experiences and insecurities. Plus, opinions can change in different situations and circumstances. What someone thinks of you today might not be the same as what they think of you tomorrow. And someone might have different opinions of you depending on the context or situation. For example, a friend might think highly of you as a person but might not agree with some of your opinions or actions.

Instead of letting other people's opinions control how you feel, focus on your own thoughts and feelings about yourself. Be confident in yourself and your abilities. Your worth is not determined by other people's opinions. Rather than looking for validation from others, find it in yourself. Focus on your own thoughts and feelings about yourself instead of letting other people's opinions control how you feel. Be confident in yourself and your abilities. Your worth is not determined by what others think of you. Find validation in yourself by setting and achieving your own personal goals and being true to who you are. It's not as simple as just disregarding other people's opinions. Yes, opinions can be subjective and change, so it's not always smart to give too much importance to what others think of you. However, social norms and other people's opinions can still affect our lives in areas such as personal relationships, school, and work. So while it's not necessary to always be concerned about what others think, it's still important to be conscious of social norms and to act respectfully and considerately towards others. The balance lies in being true to yourself while also being mindful of how your actions may affect others.

CHAPTER 5

SKILLS NEEDED IN AN EVOLVING MARKETPLACE

The world is changing rapidly, and after the 1990s, each decade is becoming increasingly different from the past decade at a faster pace. This is due to the quick advancement of technology, which has been the driving force behind many changes in recent years. This can be seen in areas such as transportation, communication, medicine, and entertainment. With new technologies like artificial intelligence, and 5G networks emerging, it is expected that the pace of change will only continue to pick up.

If you are between the ages of 25 and 30, you need to start developing skills for both the world we live in today and the world that's yet to come. In this section, we'll talk about what it takes to be successful in the real world in the coming years.

The Importance Of Common Sense For Everything:

You might have heard the saying that "common sense is no longer common," and there's some truth to it. Without common sense, you are going to struggle with life in general. Common sense refers to practical knowledge and understanding that is expected of you. In today's complex and rapidly changing world, some believe that common sense is becoming less common as the information and knowledge needed to navigate life become more specialized and diverse.

Overall, common sense is an important tool for making informed decisions and navigating the complexities of daily life. It can be developed and improved through learning and gaining new experiences.

When it comes to people, common sense and emotional intelligence are important. Have you ever met someone who is unpleasant to be around, either because they talk too much, get too emotional too soon, get angry, or are just not pleasant in general? This often stems from a lack of emotional intelligence and common sense. Common sense involves using good judgment, practicality, and the ability to think and act in a given situation. When it comes to communicating with others, using common sense can help you be more respectful, considerate, and effective in your interactions. In this section, we will examine how common sense can enhance your communication skills and help you build positive and meaningful relationships with others. Common sense plays a crucial role in life, work, and career. It helps in making informed decisions and navigating the complexities of everyday life. With common sense, one is able to approach situations and problems with practicality, good judgment, and sensibility. Whether in personal relationships or in the workplace, common sense can lead to more effective communication, better decision-making, and, ultimately, success in both personal and professional aspects of life. Common sense should be called uncommon sense since a lot of people don't have it; it is not really that common. You, on the other one, after reading this, will be aware of its importance and apply it to your own life.

Employers value common sense in both life and the workplace. it is a valuable asset that can greatly impact the success of an individual and the company as a whole. Employers are so used to people having no common sense they are too tired of it, and when they meet someone that has the ability to understand their business and their situation, they really value it. Common sense involves using good judgment, practicality, and the ability to think and act in the workplace. This translates to the ability to make informed decisions, solve problems effectively, and navigate the complexities of work.

Here are a few tips that may help you develop and use common sense in your daily life and in the marketplace

- Be observant and aware: Pay attention to your surroundings and be aware of the potential consequences of your actions. This will help you make more informed decisions and avoid potential mistakes. Be observant and aware: You want to be aware of your surroundings, where you are, and what is the situation you are going thru and behave accordingly. If you are going to be in a job interview, you want to make sure that you are ready to act accordingly and answer questions instead of not behaving in a way that is going to be acceptable to your future employer. That is just an example, and you may think that you would never act or do such a thing, but you would be amazed at the number of people with zero common sense who just do and act as they please without regard for anything. People like that do poorly in life.
- Be Proactive: Proactivity means taking the initiative to address potential problems before they occur. Make sure you are not surprised when things happen if you were doing things that made it happen. Anticipate potential

issues and take steps to prevent them rather than waiting for problems to arise before taking action. By being proactive, you can avoid problems and make more positive contributions to your work and life.

- Communicate Effectively: We talked about social skills in the previous chapter. Effective communication is the key to building positive relationships and understanding others. This involves expressing your thoughts and ideas clearly and actively listening to others. Good communication skills can help you understand and be understood by others; when you are able to do this, you will be more of an asset for yourself and a potential employer.

- Show Responsibility: Responsibility means taking ownership of your actions and decisions. This involves being accountable for what you do, admitting your mistakes, and learning from them. When you show responsibility like this, you can learn from your mistakes and make better choices in the future, building trust and credibility with others.

- Be Flexible: Flexibility means being open to change and being willing to adapt to new situations. This involves being able to adapt to new circumstances and trying new things. When you are flexible, you can be more resilient and successful in a dynamic marketplace where change is inevitable. Flexibility allows you to navigate challenges and opportunities with greater ease and make the most of new opportunities.

Digital Literacy:

No matter your life goals, whether it's starting your own venture or landing a great job working for someone else, you will need to have a strong grasp of computers and the internet. Digital literacy is about being proficient in technology and the internet. Being able to learn how to use different systems and the internet effectively. It encompasses a range of skills, such as using computers and software programs, navigating the web, and communicating online.

Digital literacy is crucial in today's world, where technology permeates both our work and leisure time. In the future, it will only become more important in the job market. Many current and future job opportunities will require the use of technology and the internet to accomplish tasks and communicate with others. Possessing strong digital literacy skills can make you more attractive to employers and improve your job performance. Additionally, digital literacy provides access to a wealth of information and resources for learning and personal growth.

Here are a few examples of digital literacy skills and the basic systems and skills you may need to have in order to use them effectively:

Email: When it comes to digital literacy in email. It involves the ability to send, receive, and organize emails efficiently. To effectively use email, you need to be familiar with a computer or other device, an internet connection, and an email client such as Microsoft Outlook or Gmail. Adapting to different email platforms and being able to communicate and respond in a timely manner. Email is very important regardless of what you do. You will use it and need it.

Social Media: Digital literacy related to social media requires the ability to create and manage social media accounts, post content, and engage with others online. And at the same time, understand how you should behave with your social media to achieve your desired outcome.

Word Processing: Basic digital literacy in word processing involves the ability to create, edit, and format documents using a word processor such as Microsoft Word or Google Docs. Basically, being able to use it for whatever your tasks are.

Online Search: Being proficient in online search means having the skills to effectively use search engines, understand search results, and critically evaluate the information found. This involves the ability to craft effective search queries, navigate search results, and determine the relevance and reliability of the information found. Online search is useful in a wide range of industries and daily life situations, as it provides access to a vast amount of information and resources. For example, it can be used for research purposes, finding information on specific products or services, locating job opportunities, and staying up-to-date on current events.

In daily life, an online search can be applied in a variety of ways, such as finding recipes, researching travel destinations, or searching for health information. Having good online search skills can help you save time and make informed decisions by quickly locating the information you need. Additionally, being able to effectively evaluate the information found through online searches can help you avoid misinformation and make more informed decisions.

What employers value

If you're thinking of being in the job market, whether in the meantime while you are doing your side project or you are there to stay, you gotta make yourself valuable. When you're working for someone or doing your own thing, you have to bring value. A good thing that employers value is that you know about what they are trying to accomplish, and you are there to help them get there. By showing that you have what they want, you'll make yourself a more attractive hire. it is one of the best ways to stand out. They are hiring you because they want to achieve something/ get something done;

show them you are the correct person for the job by understanding their business and their long-term goals.

You can highlight those skills on your resume and cover letter and focus your job search on positions that want those skills.

The four thighs all employers are going to be looking for:

Adaptability: In today's rapidly changing world, the ability to adapt to new situations and learn quickly is crucial. It involves being open-minded, willing to try new things, and quickly acquiring new skills and knowledge. This skill is important for individuals in any field, as technology, markets, and social changes are continuously evolving. They are doing it at a pace that seems to be going faster and faster. Being adaptable allows you to be ready for new opportunities and handle change with resilience.

Problem-solving: The skill of thinking creatively and finding solutions to complex problems is highly valued in a variety of careers. Being able to "think outside the box" it is a valuable skill that not a lot of people have. Problem-solving involves analyzing situations, identifying problems, and coming up with effective solutions. This skill is crucial for individuals in fields such as business, engineering, and technology, as well as many other fields where problem-solving is a key aspect of the job.

Customer service: With numerous businesses available, customers have numerous options to choose from. To stand out and retain customers, companies must provide top-notch customer service. This involves being responsive and helpful and going above and beyond to solve any issues that may arise. Good customer service can be the deciding factor for customers when choosing between businesses, so it's worth putting in extra effort to get it right. Companies with great customer service are able to keep bringing customers in even if they make mistakes sometimes.

Communication: Effective communication, both in writing and in person, is crucial for success in the modern world. You are going to be writing and talking. Do both effectively. Express yourself clearly and effectively and to understand and respond to the needs of others. This skill is important for individuals in fields such as marketing, sales, and customer service, as well as many other fields where communication is a key aspect of the job.

Collaboration: The ability to work effectively with others and contribute to a team is important in many careers. It involves working well with others, sharing ideas and knowledge, and contributing to the success of a team. This skill is crucial for individuals in fields such as management, engineering, and technology, as well as many other fields where teamwork is a key aspect of the job.

Understanding your employer's goals and mission is crucial for success in the workplace. It demonstrates a strong work ethic and dedication to the company's success. Employers seek to hire individuals who are invested in the success of the business and willing to go above and beyond to contribute to it. If you are able to show this, especially with medium size businesses that are trying to increase profits, they are going to love you. By understanding how your role fits into the bigger picture and how your work can contribute to the company's overall objectives, you can be more motivated and engaged in your work and feel a sense of purpose and fulfillment in your job. Additionally, this can make you a more valuable and effective employee, as you will be able to align your efforts with the company's needs and priorities.

Job Market Research:

Whatever career path you desire to pursue, you will need to understand the job market, especially in your city or the city you want to live. Your city or local area will have a significant impact on job availability and market conditions, but it is also essential to take a more holistic approach to market research to get a comprehensive understanding of your career prospects. This applies whether you plan to start your own business, become a lawyer, or work in real estate. Understanding industry trends, job market conditions, and the supply and demand for specific roles can help you make informed decisions about your career path.

For example, if you're interested in a career in high demand, you may have more job opportunities and a better chance of finding a job that aligns with your interests and skills. On the other hand, if you're considering a career that is in low demand, it may be more challenging to find job opportunities, and you may need to consider additional training or education to make yourself more marketable.

Job hunting can be overwhelming and frustrating, but we're here to make it as painless as possible. We'll be sharing tips and tricks we've learned along the way.

The Most Popular Websites To Find Jobs:

GOOGLE: The popular search engine also offers a job search feature. You can look for job openings by using keywords, selecting the industry and location, or just typing prompts like "Jobs in my city" and "Jobs in Denver." Prompts like this will show various job opportunities from multiple sources like job boards and company websites. Google for Jobs also lets you filter job postings based on the job type, experience level, and schedule. It even provides job alerts to stay updated on new job openings that fit your search criteria. So it will show you jobs from anywhere, and it is one of my favorite job search engines because I will search the internet for jobs that may be available for a company but are not on job boards. It has become a valuable tool for job seekers, as it aggregates job openings from various sources, making it easier to find job opportunities in one place.

INDEED: is one of the most widely used job search engines that provides job postings from various sources such as job boards, newspapers, and company websites. You can search for job openings using keywords, location, and industry, and it also lets you refine your search by date posted, company, and job title. It is one of the most popular ones and typically one of the places you want to start your search. You can filter your search by job types, such as full-time, part-time, contract, or internship, and also apply filters, such as salary, experience level, and education level.

LINKEDIN: This is a professional networking site that also offers a job search feature. You can search for job openings by using keywords, location, and industry. It lets you apply for jobs directly through the site and provides insights into the companies you're applying to and their employees.

GLASS DOOR: This is a job search website that provides job postings from multiple sources, company reviews, salary information, and interview questions for many job listings.

CRAIGSLIST: Is a classified advertisement website that has a wide range of categories, including job postings. You can find job openings by searching the "jobs" category and then filtering the results by location, industry, and job type. If you search the job listing "General Labor," it will provide you with many jobs available for immediate hire. This is something that you want to do more if you need something quick but you don't want to find something long-term. Small businesses and individual employers often use it to post job openings, making it a good source for finding local job opportunities. Be cautious, as not all job postings on Craigslist are legitimate.

ZipRecruiter: This allows you to search for jobs by using keywords, location, and industry. It also provides a free resume upload service that matches your resume to job postings. While ZipRecruiter can be a useful tool for job hunting, make sure you use it as a complement to the other tools.

If you are interested in a company, you should also check its website to see if they have any job openings. Many companies have their own career pages where they post job openings, and sending them a direct message thru their contact page is an excellent way to get their attention. It is normal if you feel overwhelmed and worried about your job research. The most common method of getting overwhelmed is being all over the place and applying everywhere. Don't do that. Get specific: instead of applying to every job under the sun, focus on a particular field or industry you're interested in. It will make your job search a lot easier. Many job search websites exist, but you don't have to use them all. That's why I didn't give you a lot more because I want you to focus on the most popular ones and make your job search more manageable.

You will need a resume. Tailoring your resume to the job you are applying for is a good idea. Tailoring your resume to the specific job and employer can increase your chances of getting an interview and ultimately getting the job. So have a main one and make different tweaks and changes that appeal more to the company you are applying for. Do not exaggerate or falsify any information on your resume. Just emphasize the most relevant experiences and skills.Some employers will contact your past employers and research you. Emphasize your most relevant experiences and skills to make your resume stand out.

<u>Here are some extra tips that you will need:</u>

- Include specific achievements: Instead of just listing your responsibilities in previous jobs, highlight specific accomplishments and quantify them with numbers when possible.
- Create a professional email address: Use a professional email address that includes your name, such as "johndoe@gmail.com," instead of an unprofessional one like "johndoe69@gmail.com."
- Update your online presence: Make sure your LinkedIn profile is up-to-date and professional, as many employers will look at your online presence.
- Research the company: Before the interview, research the company and the position you are applying for to show that you are genuinely interested and have a good understanding of the company's mission, values, and products or services.
- Prepare answers to common interview questions: Get ready for common interview questions such as "Why do you want to work here?" and "What are your strengths and weaknesses?"
- Dress accordingly: Dress appropriately for the interview, aiming for semi-formal attire, which is considered less formal than business attire but still more dressed up than casual wear.
- Bring copies of your resume: Bring copies of your resume to the interview, as well as any relevant certificates or references.
- Follow up after the interview: Send a thank-you note or email to the interviewer to express your appreciation for their time and reiterate your interest in the position. This

can help keep you top of mind and demonstrate your eagerness for the role.

MISTAKE# 7 Making Life All About Flaunting:

Many young people want to draw attention and feel good by showing off what they have and bragging about the good life they enjoy. Many teens spend a lot of money just buying expensive clothes, sneakers, shoes, cars, or other things that they can't afford to impress people they don't care about. Only to look fashionable when you have no money in the bank. Don't make the mistake of making your whole life about showing off. It is possible that without realizing you are making this mistake. Some people are just addicted to that validation. This can manifest in behaviors such as bragging, flaunting, and trying to appear perfect or always successful, which can mess up your relationships, harm your self-esteem, and at the same time, increase your levels of narcissism. You also make yourself appear superficial, which can hold you back from advancing your goals. When you're too focused on impressing others and flaunting your stuff, you're not putting your energy toward what truly matters to you. Remember, true self-worth comes from within, not from what others think of you. So, don't be someone who goes broke trying to impress others; it's not worth it.

Understanding How The World Works:

Discussing a complex and multifaceted topic like how the world works can be challenging as it involves various interconnected elements. Understanding the world can be a daunting task, but I'll do my best to explain it to you.

Every decision we make, regardless of its size, can have a significant impact on our future and shape the course of our lives. It's crucial to keep in mind that our choices can have ripple effects that go beyond our immediate circumstances. Recognizing this can assist us in making better decisions and navigating the ever-evolving world around us.

Potential life goals you may have:

- Pursuing a career or profession that you are passionate about
- Achieving financial stability and independence
- Living life on your own terms
- Building meaningful relationships with friends and loved ones
- Finding personal fulfillment and happiness
- Having the opportunity to travel and experience new cultures
- Making a positive impact on the world in some way
- Being in good health
- Have a family

Our choices about our education and career will significantly impact our future opportunities and prospects. The same goes for our personal relationships, financial decisions, and how we spend our time and energy. Having knowledge and taking action together can make a big difference in our lives and the world around us. Time and action are essential tools to help us create the future we want.

Taking action gets us into situations, and those situations take us to places where we will be in a different positions in the future. So you create your reality by what you do every day. To give you an example, researching jobs in your present will guide you to have a job in the near future. So when your future becomes the present moment, you will be in a job because of the action taken when in the past, you were in your present moment. Reread it if you did not fully grasp it

All we have is the present moment, and the actions we take today will be the past tomorrow, but they can shape the direction of our lives and determine the kind of future we will have. The habits we form today, such as exercising, saving money, or learning new skills, can have a long-term impact on our lives. We can shape our future by being mindful of how we use our time and taking deliberate action toward our goals.

We must think about how every decision we make can shape our future. Even though we can't predict the outcome of every decision, we can make choices that align with our goals and priorities. No need to stress about being perfect; we all make mistakes and have setbacks from time to time. Instead, focus on making progress and doing your best every day. Remember, success isn't always about reaching our goals overnight; it's often the result of small steps progressively over time. By focusing on our progress and setting goals, we'll be able to achieve a sense of success and fulfillment in our life.

Life is a complex and multifaceted journey shaped by many factors. The concepts of life, wealth, love, and happiness are all essential elements that contribute to a good and fulfilling life. Health is a crucial aspect of life and should be included in the list of essential concepts. Without good health, enjoying wealth, love, and happiness can be difficult. Good physical and mental health allows us to have the energy and ability to pursue our passions, build meaningful relationships, and contribute positively to the world.

Wealth is substantial because it gives us the resources and means to live a comfortable and secure life, and it is an essential tool to get what we want. It allows access to what we need and want, such as food, shelter, healthcare, and education. It also gives us the financial freedom to pursue our passions and goals. Love is essential to life as it provides us with the emotional support and connection needed to thrive. Whether it's the love of a romantic partner, family, friends, or community, having people who care for us and support us is good for our mental and social life and is one of the pillars of the good life.

Happiness is perhaps the most elusive of the four concepts. Happiness is the contentment and satisfaction of living a fulfilling and meaningful life. It's the sense of joy and purpose that we get from pursuing our passions, building meaningful relationships, and positively impacting the world. When all these elements come together, they can provide a sense of balance and fulfillment in life. So you need to balance these pillars of health, wealth, love, and happiness, as they are all interrelated. The most important thing is to focus on making progress and doing your best every day. Show up, do your best, and call it a day. Since all we have is the present and tomorrow it will be another day. Do your best today and call it a day. And tomorrow, do the same.

CHAPTER 6

FINDING YOUR OWN VERSION OF SUCCESS

Here are some quotes about success that might inspire you:

"Success is not final, failure is not fatal: It is the courage to continue that counts." - *Winston Churchill*

"The only limit to our realization of tomorrow will be our doubts of today." - *Franklin D. Roosevelt*

"Your work is going to fill a large part of your life, and the only way to be truly satisfied is to do what you believe is great work. And the only way to do great work is to love what you do." - *Steve Jobs*

"Success is walking from failure to failure with no loss of enthusiasm." - *Winston Churchill*

"Success is not how high you have climbed, but how you make a positive difference to the world." - *Roy T. Bennett*

"The road to success and the road to failure are almost exactly the same." - *Colin R. Davis*

"Success is not measured by what you accomplish, but by the opposition, you have encountered, and the courage with which you have maintained the struggle against overwhelming odds."
- *Orison Swett Marden*

"Success is the sum of small efforts, repeated day in and day out."
- *Robert Collier*

"If you want to live a happy life, tie it to a goal, not to people or things." - *Albert Einstein*

"Success is a journey, not a destination. The doing is often more important than the outcome." - *Arthur Ashe*

"The starting point of all achievement is desire." - *Napoleon Hill*

Defining What Success Means For You:

When it comes to success, everyone has their own idea of what it means. For some, it might be climbing the corporate ladder and making a ton of money. For others, it might be raising a happy family, and for others, it might be traveling the world; for others having their business, and maybe for some, a little of all of those things. The point is that success is a personal and subjective concept that can look different for each person, so it can come in many forms. You don't have to be a millionaire or a CEO to be successful. You can find success in your relationships, hobbies, career, or personal growth. The key is to figure out what success means to you and work towards it. For you, it might be a combination of several factors. It could be achieving financial stability and being able to afford the lifestyle you want, whether that means living in a particular place, owning a certain type of home, or being able to afford certain luxuries. Success might also be about your career and achieving the goals you've set for yourself in your professional life. It could be about making a positive impact on the world and leaving a legacy, whether through your work or personal endeavors. Ultimately, success is about finding personal fulfillment and happiness, which looks different for everyone."

Answering these questions will help you figure out what success means to you:

What are your long-term goals and aspirations? This refers to whatever you are trying to achieve in the long term.

- What are the most important things in your life?
- What do you want to achieve in your personal life, and what do you want to achieve professionally?
- How do you envision your future, and what role does success play in that vision?
- Where do you want to be living? Do you want to live in the city where you are right now or somewhere else, maybe in another country or multiple places?
- What is your ideal income level?
- What role do love and relationships play in your definition of success?
- How important is your social life and connections with others to your overall sense of success?
- What do you envision your life looking like in 10-20 years?
- What are your values and priorities in life?
- What are your passions and interests?
- What does success mean to you? Some people say it means making a lot of money, while others say it means traveling, achieving financial independence, or getting married and having children. What does it mean to you?

Considering these questions, you can envision the life you desire for yourself in the next 5-10 years. This will make it easier for you to identify your version of success and select the paths that will lead you in that direction. If you are reading this, your are around 17-21 years old. You have time on your side, so do not rush big moves when uncertainty is high. When facing uncertainty, it can be tempting to rush into big decisions in an effort to gain clarity or control. However, this approach can often lead to poor decision-making and negative outcomes. If you take a look at the free gift this book had for you, you will find many careers that you could consider. Lack of information can lead to poor decisions: If you make a big decision based on incomplete or inaccurate information, you may end up with a negative outcome. Taking the time to gather as much information as possible can help you make a more informed decision. More certainty can lead to better decisions.

When you have more information and are more certain about the potential outcomes of a decision, you are more likely to make a good decision that aligns with your goals and values.

MISTAKE#8 Not Understanding Failure And Giving Up Too Easily

One common mistake that people make is giving up too easily when they encounter setbacks or failures. When things don't go as planned, it can be easy to give up and think it's the end of the road. But that's not how it works; failure is just a part of the journey, and it plays a role in success. Failure is simply feedback that can be used to learn and grow. Failure is a part of life, and it's something that everyone experiences at some point. It is not a reflection of your worth or your abilities, it is simply a setback or feedback that can help you learn and grow. The idea is that when you fail, you gain valuable information about what didn't work and can use that knowledge to improve and try again. Failure can also lead to personal growth and help individuals to develop resilience, grit, and determination. It can also be a powerful motivator that allows individuals to focus on their goals and take action to achieve them.

It is an inevitable part of trying to achieve anything worthwhile. We learn and grow through failure, and it is often through overcoming setbacks and failures that we find success; rather than giving up when things don't go as planned, just learn what doesn't work to get there.

By understanding that failure is a normal and necessary part of the process, you can learn to embrace it rather than letting it discourage you. Many people give up too easily because they don't understand how failure works, and they see failure as a sign of weakness or as a confirmation that they can't succeed. Instead of giving up after a failure, take a step back, reassess the situation, and try again.

Kickstarting Your Career:

Are you ready to embark on the exciting journey of kickstarting your career? It can be overwhelming to think about where to begin, but with a clear vision of your goals and a little bit of planning, you'll be on your way to where you want to be. As I said before, by thinking about where you want to be in the next 5-10 years, you can start to map out a plan to make it happen. In this text, I'll give you some tips to consider when you're ready to kickstart your career. We've got some great tips for anyone who's looking to start their career, no matter what they want to do or whether they're going to college or not. These tips are for anyone wanting to succeed and take control of their future. Of course, everyone's journey is different, so not all tips will work for everyone. But by following them, you can lay a solid foundation for your career and achieve your goals. Whether you already know what you want to do or you're still figuring things out, these tips will help you stay motivated and on track. So get ready to take these tips on board and start your exciting journey toward a successful and fulfilling career!

Renting an apartment or house and finding roommates:

Finding a place to live that suits your budget and preferences is crucial in kickstarting your career. You probably don't want to live with your parents, which is normal. Consider factors such as location, amenities, and cost when searching for a rental. Deciding whether to live alone or with roommates is another critical consideration. Living with roommates can save on rent and utility costs but also brings challenges, such as coordinating schedules and dealing with potential conflicts. Once you've found a place, you'll need to review and sign a lease and be prepared to deal with any issues that may arise with your landlord or roommates. it can be difficult to find an apartment with bad credit. Most landlords and property managers will perform a credit check as part of the application process, and a low credit score can make it harder to be approved for an apartment. Landlords may view bad credit as an indication that you are not financially responsible, making them hesitant to rent to you.

In some cases, landlords may require a co-signer, a higher security deposit, or proof of income to compensate for poor credit. One way to go around this is to be upfront about your credit situation and communicate with the landlord to show that you are responsible and capable of paying rent on time. Review the lease carefully, understand your rights and responsibilities as a tenant, and have a plan to deal with potential problems.

<u>Many websites can help you find apartments and roommates. Here are some of the best websites to check out:</u>

1. **Zillow:** Zillow is a popular real estate website that lists apartments and houses for rent. You can filter your search by location, price, and number of bedrooms and see photos and descriptions of each property.

2. **Apartments.com:** Apartments.com is another popular website for finding apartments. It features a variety of search filters, including pet-friendly options and amenities like parking, laundry, and fitness centers.

3. **Roomster:** Roomster is a website that helps you find roommates. You can create a profile, search for potential roommates, and message them directly through the site.

4. **Roomi:** Roomi is another roommate-finding website that lets you search for roommates based on location, budget, and lifestyle. You can chat with potential roommates through the site and even pay rent through the Roomi platform.

5. **Craigslist:** Craigslist is a classified website that can be a good resource for finding apartments and roommates. Be cautious when using Craigslist, however, and take steps to verify that the listing or the person you're communicating with is legitimate.

6. **PadMapper:** PadMapper is a website that aggregates apartment listings from other sites, making it easy to browse a variety of options in one place. You can also set up alerts to be notified when new apartments meeting your criteria become available.

7. **Facebook Marketplace:** You can search for rentals and roommates on Facebook Marketplace by location, price,

and number of bedrooms, and also filter your search by amenities, pet policy, and more. This is a great option for finding rentals and roommates within your own social network.

8. **Google:** You can also search for rentals and roommates on Google by using relevant keywords such as "apartments for rent near me" or "roommates wanted in (city name)". This can be a great way to find listings that aren't on larger rental and roommate-matching websites.

Expenses that you are likely to have:

Rent or mortgage: This is typically one of the largest expenses for people, and it covers the cost of housing, whether you own or rent your home.

Utilities: This includes expenses such as electricity, gas, water, and internet.

Transportation: This includes expenses such as car payments, insurance, maintenance, and fuel. If you don't own a car, you may also have public transportation expenses.

Groceries: This includes the cost of buying food and household items.

Credit card payments: This includes payments on credit card balances.

Entertainment: This includes expenses such as dining out, movies, going out with friends, and other leisure activities.

College expenses: This can include tuition, room and board, books, and supplies.

Cell phone and internet: Teens often have expenses related to owning and using a cell phone, as well as internet service.

So with all these expenses, you need to support yourself while you build your desired lifestyle. The best advice that I have for you is to get a job that is similar or related to your desired future career. This can help you gain experience in the field and develop the skills and knowledge you need to succeed in that career. It's worth noting that not all jobs are similar or related to your desired career, but it will give you the experience and exposure you need to move forward. It empowers your future path.

To optimize and prepare your routine for your goals, consider the following steps:

Define your goals: Identify what you want to achieve, and make sure your goals are specific, measurable, and realistic.

Evaluate your current routine: Take a look at your current routine and evaluate what works and what doesn't. Consider what changes you need to make to align your routine with your goals.

Prioritize your tasks: Determine which tasks are most important for achieving your goals, and prioritize those tasks in your routine.

Plan your day/week: Plan your day or week in advance, taking into account your most important tasks and scheduling them at the most optimal times.

Create a structured routine: Create a structured routine that supports your goals and includes time for tasks that help you achieve them. This can include things like exercise, meditation, learning new skills, and networking.

Eliminate distractions: Identify distractions that may be preventing you from achieving your goals, and take steps to eliminate them. This can include things like turning off your phone or social media notifications during certain times of the day.

Stay flexible: Remember that life is unpredictable, and be willing to adjust your routine when necessary. Be open to new opportunities and adjust your routine as needed to stay on track with your goals.

Managing your finances:

We already had a full chapter about this, so I don't want to expand too much. Achieving financial stability requires a balance of both increasing income and managing expenses. Some people have an income problem, some have a spending problem, and others have both. You need to assess your financial situation and work on finding solutions that address any issues you may face, whether increasing your income, cutting expenses or both.

Maintaining good physical and mental health:

This is crucial for overall well-being and can significantly impact financial stability. Eating a balanced diet, exercising regularly, getting enough sleep, and managing stress are essential to leading a healthy lifestyle. Taking care of your health can improve your productivity, performance and ultimately help you save money by reducing the likelihood of costly medical expenses. Mental health is just as important as physical health when leading a fulfilling life. A positive mental state can help you feel motivated, engaged and help you cope with stress and challenges. Taking care of your mental health through stress management, self-care, and seeking support when needed can help you maintain your mental well-being and enjoy life to the fullest.

Good physical and mental health are interconnected, and caring for one can improve the other. Regular exercise not only improves physical health but has been shown to positively affect mental health. Similarly, good mental health can help you make healthier choices regarding diet and exercise. When you feel good physically and mentally, you are more likely to interact positively with others and maintain healthy relationships. On the other hand, struggling with physical or mental health issues can make it difficult to maintain positive relationships with others. Therefore, taking care of your health should be a top priority for achieving overall financial stability and your goals in life.

Dealing with the challenges of being single and possibly lonely:

Being single and lonely is extremely common. In the United States and other western countries, it has become increasingly common in recent years due to various factors, such as technology and social media, which can limit face-to-face interactions, and the fast-paced nature of modern life. Loneliness can have negative effects on both physical and mental health, making it harder for people to feel fulfilled and achieve their goals. It can lead to mental health issues such as depression and anxiety and increase stress levels and feelings of disconnection from others.

Loneliness can also be expected in environments like entrepreneurship and college. These environments can be demanding and require a lot of effort and time to succeed, leaving little time for socializing and building connections with others.

However, keep in mind that spending time alone can also be a valuable experience for personal growth and self-reflection. It can provide a chance to gain a deeper understanding of oneself and one's values and space for creativity and inspiration.

Show up, Do Your Best, And Call It a Day

I have given you a lot of information in this book. it was a lot of info to take in but take your time and don't get overwhelmed. You don't have to do it all at once, and it's normal not to have all the answers.

Just take it day by day and focus on making progress. Some days will be better than others; that's just how it goes. By breaking it down into smaller steps and focusing on one step at a time, you'll be able to achieve your goal in a more manageable and less stressful way. Just get in the path of progress rather than perfection. Imperfect action is better than perfect inaction.

For example, suppose you have a career and are working towards a degree in a specific field instead of becoming overwhelmed by the thought of completing the entire program. In that case, the student can break it down into smaller goals. There is only so much you can do in a day, so relax. Each semester, the student can set a goal of getting good grades and passing all their classes. Each day, the student can focus on completing their assignments, studying for exams, and attending class.

Another example: let's say you want to get into real estate. Instead of thinking about the whole process, break it down into smaller steps. First, start learning about the business and how, little by little, you can start submerging yourself in the industry. Then, you can set a goal of getting your real estate license first, focus on finding a good broker and building your network, and start working on closing some deals. Life is a journey, and every day is an opportunity to progress, so don't get discouraged if things don't go as planned. Just keep moving forward. So take small steps every day towards your goal and if you feel like you got a lot done that day, and feel good about yourself, call it a day. Progress doesn't always have to be a huge leap or a dramatic change; it can be incremental and come from consistently taking small actions over time. The key is to focus on the process, not just the outcome, and to celebrate your small wins along the way.

Living The Life, You Want To Live

As humans, we are entitled to pursue the life we want to live, but we are not necessarily entitled to the outcome we desire. Pursuing the life we want means that we can make choices and take actions that align with our values, interests, and aspirations. It means that we have the freedom to explore different paths and opportunities and to strive towards achieving our goals. But when it comes to the outcome, it works a little differently. The following quote is attributed to Charles J. Sykes, an American author, journalist, and radio host: To get what we want, we must deserve what we want. The world is still not a crazy enough place to reward a whole bunch of underserving people". Life is a journey, and you're in it. You should strive to make the most of it, chase your dreams, pursue your passions, and work towards your goals. It may not always be easy, but the effort and determination you put into achieving your goals makes life worth living. You should not be afraid to take risks and try new things; that is how you grow and learn. The ability to try and the effort you put into your life makes you human.

You have 24 hours in a day, just like everyone else. Your life is yours to control, and you can shape it and mold it into the life you want to live using action and time. The possibilities are endless, and the only thing stopping you from achieving your dreams is yourself. But don't let that discourage you because you can achieve anything you want with hard work, persistence, and a positive attitude. It's easy to get caught up in the distractions of everyday life and let your fears and doubts hold you back. You may be tempted to give up on your goals and settle for a life that is less than what you truly want. But remember, life is too short to settle for anything less than what you truly desire. The most important thing is to pursue what makes you happy and fulfilled.

Your career is a big part of your life, and choosing one that aligns with your values, passions, and interests is important. It's important to remember that it's not always easy to find the perfect career, and it might take some trial and error to find what truly makes you happy. But ultimately, as long as you are true to yourself and putting in the effort to chase your dreams, you should not feel wrong about your chosen career path if that is what you want to do with your life.

CONCLUSION

I hope that you enjoyed reading this book as much as I enjoyed writing it. It can be hard to summarize all the skills you are going to need, but I have included the ones that will help you the most in your daily life as an adult. I hope this book has provided you with a lot of great insights and that you had many "aha" moments where you became more aware of how the world works, what to expect in life, and the basics to help you achieve your goals. I also hope you are less likely to make the mistakes I summarized in this book. The world is a complex place, There is no single, universally accepted answer to what the meaning of life is, so I hope that you believe I did a good job summarizing what you need to succeed in life in your own way. Please read the free gift that you received with the book. It is designed to give you specific information about the careers and paths you can take once you finish high school.

If there is one thing that I hope you have learned from this book, it is that success is what you make of it. That's another reason why it was challenging for me to cover all aspects of life in this book because every single person is different, and they have different goals and aspirations. But, overall, we all want the same things in life: to be happy, healthy, to have enough resources, and to live a fulfilling life. So make sure you are in the flow. Meaning knowing where you are, where you are going, and moving toward that direction. The methods to achieve these goals will be different for each person. Therefore, I have tried to be general in providing you with skills that you will need, regardless of your life goals. I hope that you will continue to read and enjoy my work. I also hope that you find the gift helpful and that it contributes to making your life easier.

Made in United States
Orlando, FL
23 October 2023

38125635R10065